Elizabeth M

DESIGN BY
DEFINITION

Publisher: Jeffrey Zeldman
Designer: Jason Santa Maria
Executive director: Katel LeDû
Editor in chief: Lisa Maria Marquis
Editors: Greg Nicholl, Caren Litherland, Susan Bond
Book producer: Ron Bilodeau

ISBN: 978-1-952616-57-0

A Book Apart
New York, New York
http://abookapart.com

10 9 8 7 6 5 4 3 2 1

TABLE OF CONTENTS

FOREWORD

THE WORD "DESIGN" YIELDS undeniable power. It can mean so many things—it's both a noun, "the design," and a verb, "we're designing." It can mean to decorate, to devise, to demarcate. It implies intention, deliberateness, and sometimes duplicity. It describes the creation of anything from physical objects to printed matter to the architecture of intangible systems, and more.

While powerful, this vast pliability can have its downsides—the practice of design as a craft can feel like a slippery slope where the boundaries of scope, responsibility, execution, and iteration are indistinct, even blurry.

And the implication here goes beyond just semantics. The lack of dialogue using concrete terms and the inability to identify discreet edges of a given design problem, can cause the derailment or undoing of countless work hours for practitioners. When a design process neglects the integration of categorical terms, then passion, effort, opportunity, and money will surely be lost.

Luckily, Elizabeth McGuane gives form to the ambiguity by showing us the power of specificity—in words, in numbers, and in images. *Design by Definition* is an invaluable collection of strategies for teasing apart design problems that are otherwise confusing, muddled, or inconstant, and translating them into clear, operable, material opportunities for designers to apply the best of their ingenuity. This book is an ode to the power of language—written, spoken, visual, and numeric language—and its ability to reveal the best of design.

—**Khoi Vinh**

INTRODUCTION

EVERY DESIGN STARTS WITH WORDS.

So many of the tools of writing—not just the words them-selves, but the craft of putting them together—echo, and are echoed in, the craft of design. So much of design is better and clearer when we understand just how much of it is tangled up in words. Designing with a writer's tools frames design as a communication problem—which it is. It's a communication problem in many directions, not just from maker to user but among the people doing the designing and building. Defining our ideas within a design project helps us understand one another as we design things together.

I've called this book *Design by Definition*—which, yes, is a pun, the lowest form of humor; but please allow it, because it's true. We design by defining the things we make. We work with ideas by describing them, by naming them, and by approaching them through metaphor and allusion. We work through user flows by considering narrative, audience, and pace. When it comes to the parts of a system, or the way we lay out infor-mation on a page, we're really working with nouns and verbs.

I come to design from a language and writing background. In design, the work I've done with words hasn't felt like writing so much as construction, or, rather, deconstruction: the pro-cess of breaking down a digital product—a website or a web app—into its parts of speech. Nouns and verbs, because they describe objects and actions—the building blocks of interaction design—have always been my scaffolding for understanding how things work.

Sometimes my work has felt like translation, or code-break-ing: trying to decode meaning from problem statements and technical documents. As a design manager, this translation most often happens as I review visual design work, decoding the ideas and systems behind an interface. (Later, I'll get into the ways we often rush to visualization without defining what we're visualizing, and why this can block us from visual paths we might otherwise have explored.)

I've worn many names and definitions in design, and I've led design teams filled with different titles: visual designers, researchers, content designers, writers, taxonomists, and more. Spending time with all those labels has shown me that design is a single concept that can be described in different ways, depending on the tools you have to hand. The outcome—the product that's brought to life from an idea—is what matters, and it needs many eyes and many chisels to make it real. So I always knew my work was design work—that articulating concepts clearly, modeling systems, and defining taxonomies and information were not just an extension of clever copywriting.

Throughout the past decade and a half, the tools I've applied to design have been a reimagining of the writing tools I brought with me. Again and again, these were the mechanics I used to decode a problem, understand a system, or structure a solution.

When you try to design something physical that has never existed before—say, a chair—at a certain point, that idea becomes something you can hold in your hands (or sit on); something built in the real world, with real materials.

When we design software products, we never really reach that point. We make digital products and features by imagining our way toward them, and our road to reality never ends with wood and metal or gears and pulleys. Instead, *words* and *images* and *numbers* are our material.

Of those, words are the material that feels the most pivotal, because we can only create in images and code what we can first describe. Those descriptions—the definitions of our ideas— shape what we make in powerful ways.

By spending some time defining our ideas and considering the impact of our words, we can embrace the power of language as a design tool. We can tighten our designs by excavating our concepts, defining them, and bringing them into sharper relief.

WORDS ARE FOR EVERYONE

You might imagine a writer's life to be a solitary one, and that's sometimes true. I felt that solitude with a shock when I started writing this book, at the tail end of a global pandemic, in the deep end of a Canadian winter. Prior to that, most of my writing had been done in pairs, in groups, and in public: I had spent the previous thirteen years working with design teams to build websites and web and mobile products, plus a few years at an old-school newsroom before that.

In writing this book, while isolated, I found myself reflecting on the ways writing can be a surprisingly group-oriented activity. I also found myself exploring interests and experiences I had in common with people who don't work in writing, or even design, at all: with engineers, product managers, and founders building brand-new products. So I hope this book is useful to anyone defining and building things collaboratively.

When we build together, it's common to run into moments when we can't clearly communicate with one another. Perhaps we've started sketching out solutions for an idea, but we don't all agree yet on what we're making. I spot this happening all the time:

- When, in design critiques, we dwell on the details of an interface, rather than on what the whole design actually communicates;
- when we disagree on names for products or features; and
- when everyone on a team seems to be aiming for a slightly different product outcome.

A hazily defined concept is often at the root of these troubles, which are experienced on every kind of design team and in every size of company.

In the process of writing this book, I learned that no matter what we're making or what our expertise might be, we all spend time in confusion over our concepts and the words we use to describe them. The tools of language are there for all of us to use to work through this confusion. I hope this book helps anyone grappling with critical moments in a product development process, no matter their background.

The ideas and tools I'm sharing are for everyone, and may even be most useful to those who don't see themselves as writers. Words are just tools, after all—and they're in the hands of visual designers, engineers, product managers, and everyone else involved in making software (or making anything, really). They're tools you can use in every project, whether you have a methodical and linear design and development process or a squiggly and roundabout one.

WHAT'S IN THIS BOOK

It's a tricky thing, writing about words. Because we must use words to describe how words work, the whole enterprise can become self-referential. To make things a bit more tangible, I've structured this book as a walk through the various stages of the design process. We'll see the ways language affects and informs product design, from the idea through to the execution of the final product:

- **Chapter 1**: Framing and unpacking the idea itself
- **Chapter 2**: Exploring the ways metaphors bring the idea to life and help collaborative teams understand it together
- **Chapter 3:** Landing on the right name
- **Chapter 4:** Placing the idea in a narrative or journey
- **Chapter 5:** Bringing the idea to life through tone, pacing, writing style, and visual expression
- **Chapter 6:** Anticipating and facing the way concepts change, and how they change the systems they're a part of

Each of these chapters is a reminder to consider what words really mean, and how differently we understand and interpret those words. The book as a whole invites you to consider the act of definition and interpretation as you begin to sketch and build your own ideas into being.

A BRIEF GLOSSARY

A few words recur throughout this book. I use them to talk about ideas and how they come to life:

- A *concept model* is a visualization of a product or a system. Having a concept model for a product, or even for features within it, ensures there's a single clear perspective that everyone understands, so that everyone working on the system can design from a common baseline.
- A *mental model* is a framework an individual person uses to understand something. Like language, mental models are often created and used unconsciously. We bring our own experiences and biases to the table to create a picture in our mind's eye.
- An *object* is a fundamental, reusable part of a system. The nature of an object depends on the system we're talking about. In a product, *objects* can include both the *users* of the product and the things they can create within it.
- A *platform* is any product that can be extended or built upon by offering a public interface (an application programming interface, or API) to external developers. Most platforms are characterized by having multiple users—the customers buying the product and the developers building on it, and possibly an end user as well.
- A *product* is a feature, or set of features, in a digital application, packaged under a single name for sales and marketing purposes. This word is often used interchangeably with *application* or *platform*, but in the context of this book, I'll be talking about products as a set of features *within* an application.
- A *system* is any connected set of concepts that work together to generate an outcome over time. Language is a system of words and rules that work together to perform communication. A design system is a set of visual and text patterns and components that work together to create a cohesive design.

I'll define other terms throughout the book as they appear—but these words are the building blocks that come up again and again.

ZOOMING OUT

Successful design often comes from a designer's ability to zoom out. Words are a great way of adjusting your design lens to give you a different perspective on a problem. Names, metaphors, and storytelling can quickly drive a wedge into any concept and open it up in novel and interesting ways. What's even better is that they're very egalitarian tools. Some of us who specialize in writing bemoan the fact that "everyone thinks they can write," worrying that writing's apparent accessibility creates a perception of lower value compared to, say, the ability to draw or sketch.

But good design doesn't come from a single skill. Some of the best visual designers I know are terrible at sketching, too. A writer's foothold in design shouldn't be limited to their ability to turn a phrase, and words are not something to gatekeep.

So I choose to see the phrase "everyone thinks they can write" a bit differently. Everyone not only can write, but *should* write—and do a lot more of it, with more intention and joy. Words are one of our most powerful, slippery, and delightfully democratic tools for understanding our ideas, ourselves, and one another. Why not get the most out of them?

HOW TO CATCH AN IDEA

FIRST OF ALL, LET'S DEFINE OUR TERMS. What exactly are we trying to catch? What is a design idea?

Every digital product starts out as a problem to be solved. The *idea*, or concept, is the way we meet that problem—the premise of our solution. These ideas can be wide-ranging in scope; they can take advantage of an existing system or invent a new one. For example, when trying to design an email product, you could rethink the nature of correspondence and email completely, or you could ground your designs in familiar, mail-related terms and concepts that people have heard before. You could explore a solution with a specific focus—designing an experience around the act of writing, say, that clears away all other distractions. Or you could design a productivity tool geared toward helping users clear out their inbox at speed.

Every problem and every design space can be met with dozens of possible solutions. And every one of those solutions needs to be described and defined on the road to being visualized and made.

Now, you might argue that a good visual design *is* its own explanation. And so it is—when it's complete. Ideally, a user shouldn't need a product glossary to understand the basics of your design. But when you're in the process of designing, you're going to need definitions. You're going to need to explain your concept to your design team, your engineers, your product manager, and any other stakeholders you meet on the road to a finished product. And you'll need, more often than you think, to describe it to yourself. When you can pin down a concept with words, you'll find you can hang onto it long enough to draw it into reality.

When you define your ideas as you work, you have a roadmap to refer to as you design your interfaces and user flows. You can be more precise in the way you talk about and understand the goals of your design. And you can stay focused on what you are trying to say.

Prototypes are great for visualizing an idea quickly, as are wireframes and other tools. But if, when it comes time to name what you've designed, you have difficulty articulating and framing it, see if you can leave space in your process for finding the edges of your idea and giving it shape.

WHAT'S A PRODUCT ABOUT?

All designers need to dig deep into the semantic parts of design, though visual designers I've spoken with have often said they lacked the language to talk about this process. Data scientists, engineers, and product managers also need well-defined terms. Engineers obsess over naming; data scientists need well-framed ideas to know what to measure; and product managers live and die by well-articulated problem statements.

It's easy to fall back on the familiar, to use language and names we've heard before, to mimic and borrow from the world around us. That's fine, and even appropriate a lot of the time. Invention is not its own reward when it comes to describing an idea. Familiar things can be easily understood, but they need to be accurate. Words carry weight, so it's important to stop and think about why a word feels appropriate to you in describing what you're making—to have a hard think about what it really means.

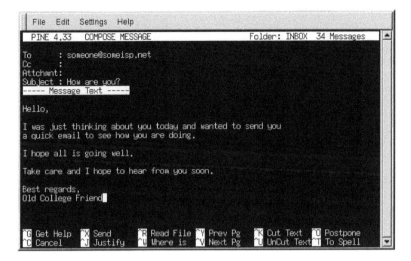

```
  File  Edit  Settings  Help
┌──────────────────────────────────────────────────────────────┐ ▲
│  PINE 4.33    COMPOSE MESSAGE              Folder: INBOX  34 Messages │
│                                                                │
│ To      : someone@someisp.net                                  │
│ Cc      :                                                      │
│ Attchmnt:                                                      │
│ Subject : How are you?                                         │
│ ----- Message Text -----                                       │
│                                                                │
│ Hello,                                                         │
│                                                                │
│ I was just thinking about you today and wanted to send you     │
│ a quick email to see how you are doing.                        │
│                                                                │
│ I hope all is going well.                                      │
│                                                                │
│ Take care and I hope to hear from you soon.                    │
│                                                                │
│ Best regards,                                                  │
│ Old College Friend█                                            │
│                                                                │
│                                                                │
│ ^G Get Help  ^X Send      ^R Read File ^Y Prev Pg  ^K Cut Text  ^O Postpone │
│ ^C Cancel    ^J Justify   ^W Where is  ^V Next Pg  ^U UnCut Text^T To Spell │
└──────────────────────────────────────────────────────────────┘ ▼
```

FIG 1.1: Pine's early interface was delightfully minimalist.

Know where you stand

I went to high school in the mid-1990s, and one of my earliest memories of interacting with a software interface was an application called Pegasus Mail. Like other tools of the same vintage (such as the email client Pine), it was extremely basic, but it contained ideas and elements that persist in similar software today (**FIG 1.1**).

Flash forward to a few years later, when I was using a more polished version of the Pegasus program on a small Mac computer, usually in the school library, writing lots of long emails and printing out the replies to take home (**FIG 1.2**).

At some point, the creators of Pegasus and other early email clients decided on a few simple visual and linguistic paradigms that have stayed with the technology ever since.

The concepts that live beneath these interfaces—folders, mailboxes, lists, and pages—have persisted from design to design. The concepts, language, and metaphors behind these designs act as an anchor, making email feel like a tool we intuitively understand.

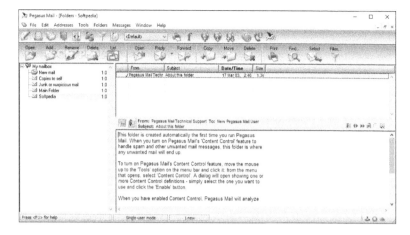

FIG 1.2: This version of Pegasus Mail (with an updated UI) is even more evocative of today's email interfaces.

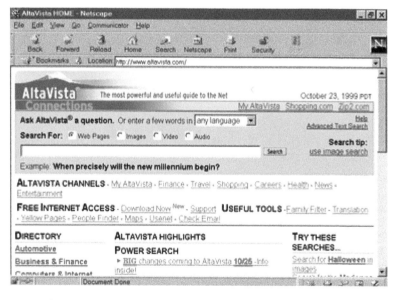

FIG 1.3: AltaVista was an early search tool whose design was all about bubbling up every category you could think of and letting you do the rest of the work.

Now imagine for a moment that you're trying to sketch out another ubiquitous technology, a service all of us use every day: a search engine. You're designing a search interface. But this search interface is a leap forward from what has come before it. It solves a problem in a unique way.

Before Google, search engines (such as AltaVista) dealt in controlled queries—you had to know how to speak their language to be able to get close to a good result (FIG 1.3).

Google's stroke of genius was that a simple, human query—even a question had a better hope of returning a good result.

This new way of solving the problem of search changed the way we all interacted with search engines, browsers, and technology in general. It changed our expectations of what software could offer. For good or ill, it made software feel a little bit more magical.

What set Google apart was a clear understanding of its idea: the concept that drove it from technology to design. Where other search engines had been catalogs of websites, listing URLs using the hierarchical file structure inspired by the nomenclature of the internet itself, Google looked at these elements as a network without hierarchy—a mesh of backlinks and cross-references.

The clarity of this idea was so well defined to its founders that it found its way into the interface design of the product. It was boldly a search input field and nothing else (FIG 1.4).

That confidence, I believe, comes from a concept that is deeply and intuitively understood by those making it. Google wasn't under any illusions about needing to copy or mimic what had come before it, and that freed the company to make bold design choices, even though it was led more by technology than design at the time.

Now, in these two examples—email and search—the important thing isn't which design idea was objectively better. Reinventing how the technology worked wasn't the only way for Google to create a good design. What matters is that those working on these different tools (email and search) understood the system they were creating. They had to know whether they were making something new or extending an architecture that had come before.

FIG 1.4: Google's early interface, full of excitement (check out that exclamation point) over the lack of category links.

Understanding your system's evolution is the first step to delivering a clear design concept that will help that system progress.

From big idea to detailed pattern

If an idea is a hard thing to pin down for an entire sector of software like search or email, it's also hard to pin down when you get into the fine details of a specific product, feature, or pattern. Understanding where design ideas come from and how to describe them matters at every level, but the work required to understand them is different. To get a handle on how this work of idea definition varies depending on scale, it helps to have a framework in mind. This framework doesn't describe the origin or purpose of every idea, but it does cover all the examples in this book.

Design ideas can appear at four levels of scale, from the macro (industry) to the micro (meaning of a visual pattern):

1. An industry or sector, such as email or search
2. A product or platform, such as Google or Facebook
3. A specific feature, like a search list or news feed
4. A distinct visual or interaction pattern within a specific product

The way ideas take shape will depend on where your attention is focused within this scale; defining ideas at each level will demand different tools. For example, defining an entirely new product—like Google's search innovation in the 1990s—was a different job than defining a new search feature today. But it's still important to define what "search" is and what it's becoming as we choose how to represent that evolution in a modern interface.

Throughout this book, I'll focus on examples from across this scale, but will pay most attention to ideas that shape products and specific features.

WORDS MEAN THINGS

English-language dictionaries have been around for centuries. In 1604, Robert Cawdrey published *A Table Alphabeticall*, considered the first dictionary in English (https://bkaprt.com/dd46/01-01).

Early dictionaries defined words that were relatively new or complex, that borrowed from other languages, or that referenced new concepts. Today, one might assume that a dictionary exists to set and keep standards, and that certain words should be excluded because they're deemed "unreal" in some way. But dictionaries exist to observe, rather than to judge. They collect and analyze how we use, make, and remake words—pointing out not just what's new about the way we communicate, but also how our words evolve. So if words easily shift their meanings in the day-to-day world, how do they change in the digital realm, and how do those changes affect how we design?

Unpacking an idea

In product companies, design happens in groups. Not only do design reviews often take the form of a panel, with feedback coming from many stakeholders; but designers also often pair up as they design, working with other designers during exploration and execution, and with engineers and product managers when framing the problem they're solving and how to solve it.

Each team member's mental model of a concept includes not just the words they use to describe it, but the story they tell about it. The way they relate one part of a model to another, their starting point in describing it, and how much focus they bring to one part over another—all of these are part of someone's constructed mental model. Because mental models are individual and subjective, they can be influenced, but they can't be entirely supplanted—they'll always include a little bit of beautiful subjective mess.

When we work together, we assume that others will understand the words we use to describe our work—we're quick to assume a shared mental model. We also mimic the words we hear others use, though we might understand them differently. We're social animals, and we copy one another, borrowing scraps like magpies. We do this to reach across a communication divide and to integrate ourselves into a culture, performing a mimicry of the words used around us. And because we can only speak and design from our own mental models, we will misunderstand one another unless we actively discuss and externalize those models.

A team either comes up with a proposal for a new feature or product or receives a dictate from higher up to build one. Team members may have an idea. They spend time discussing the idea, usually in a formal document, and then begin to design and prototype. Along the way, disagreements spin up. Meetings last longer than they should and feel unproductive, as team members disagree about the purpose and intent of their project. Still later, when the team examines an interface design, the labels applied to elements of the design come under frequent discussion, as do their place in the information hierarchy of a page or a workflow. Engineers debate with designers about whether terminology in their APIs should also appear in the user-facing design. There is a constant sense of micromanagement. Team members muddle along and eventually wrangle their interface into something that most of them accept as reality.

The first job of unpacking an idea is to figure out what the current and past mental models are. How do people—all sorts of people—think about and understand the system you're designing for?

The goal of defining, analyzing, and making an idea concrete is not to mire a design in endless discussion. The goal of reaching a consistent concept model is not to shout down opposing points of view. Instead, we can discover ideas through various forms of qualitative research.

The aim of any qualitative research is to cast a light on different points of view, whether that means finding out what your users think or surfacing your colleagues' mental models. It's important to do this work early on in a project to ensure the least amount of friction and wasted time. And the type of output you get from this research matters. A good trick is to focus on artifacts that externalize people's mental models and ways of thinking by having them sketch or diagram how they see a problem. A recorded discussion alone is great, but sketches—because they're abstractions, and because they hint at notions a person might not have been able to express outright—can give you something meaningful to respond to in your next design iteration.

The most ubiquitous form of qualitative research is, of course, the user interview. But it can be difficult to get user insight into an idea you've yet to bring to life. Users may be able to give you insight into a problem that your product could solve, or they might describe their mental model for using tools that are like the ones you plan to build. But if you want to avoid the anxiety of influence, you need to bring users some sort of design artifact to respond to. It's best to talk to them when your idea is a bit more real. Desk research and mental-model exploration are useful for clarifying the idea you're crafting before it reaches your audience. Two reliable methods for doing that include content audits and drawing and sketching, which we'll look at next.

Auditing everything

Throughout my career, I have gotten deep satisfaction from building spreadsheets and conducting audits. Something about the process of neatly cataloging every part of a system—its objects and actions, its users and content—soothes my soul.

You can audit a product in various ways—by digging for nuances of style or visual variation, or by looking for issues involving accessibility or performance. What I tend to do, especially when I'm new to a design team, is audit what a product is about. I try to unpack its nature. And the best way I know how to do this is by cataloging its nouns and verbs.

A linguistic audit of a system is a powerful starting point for building something new, and it's deceptively simple. *Nouns* and *verbs*, those two little parts of speech, encompass so much about digital space because they describe *objects* and *actions*. Understanding them builds a scaffolding for understanding everything else.

Once you've audited your product and listed everything it could possibly contain, your work is just beginning. Auditing is satisfying, and color-coding a spreadsheet is delightful—but there's a falseness to the clean columns and rows you've created. No two-dimensional audit can capture every dimension of a system, and an audit's aura of completeness is misleading. Every audit carries the bias of its author. You've had to choose how to categorize things and how to group things, and that will influence the patterns you find in your finished survey.

Still, if you know what you're looking for and can temper your findings with a bit of humility (you're bound to find some hidden section of functionality that eluded you on your first survey), it's a great place to start. An audit can uncover unexpected richness and nuance in a system. I've often started an audit simply to learn about the product I was working on, to see what features were used across the system. But in cataloging a system, I would find discrepancies and confusion in its organizing principles and labeling decisions. Often I'd find accidental associations between two features that bore no obvious connection.

Cataloging an interface, then, is a great starting point for understanding what a system is trying to express, and for measuring the delta between that and what it is *really* expressing.

Revelations through sketching

When a company is in its early stages, a lot of time can be spent defining what the product it's making actually does—all part of the fun of finding product market fit. It's an existential time for a company, which is what makes it such an exciting time for a linguistically oriented person. Everything is about meaning, and every meaning is up for debate.

When I joined the messaging startup Intercom, the company was out of that early stage and enjoying success, but was still best known for the little message icon you still see in the corners of many websites that lets users directly message companies and reach real humans on the other side. Intercom had drawn its inspiration from consumer messaging, and was determined to make communication with businesses feel more human.

At the time I came onboard, the engineering team was calling for a content specialist to help refine names and concepts. Together, we declared a principle: *The same language from code to customer.* This meant using the same language in code that we used in the product experience. I later learned the pitfalls of such an aim, but the goal—of consistency and clarity—was laudable.

The company asked me to help them with naming certain features, so I began to explore all the terminology used within the company—in the form of documentation, APIs, support conversation logs, and so on—with the intention of making a glossary that defined every feature. I set up interviews with people across the company in every department, from sales and support to design, engineering, and product. I also did desk research by looking through every support document, blog post, and internal document I could find, to establish a baseline—if there was one—that told me where certain terms came from.

FIG 1.5: This sketch, one of many produced by our interviewees, shows a mental model of Intercom that puts people—the product's users—front and center. (The hearts represent the wish fulfillment of happy customers.)

A researcher and I conducted these staff interviews together. We didn't sit down with a list of words and ask people to define them. Instead, we held thirty-minute sessions where we asked people to describe the product to others, ending with what became the most enlightening part of the study: a sketching exercise.

We instructed each person to draw their idea of the product just as they thought of it, giving them no further guidance. Some people sketched images that highlighted how the product helped its users (**FIG 1.5**). Others drew diagrams of the code itself. Each response was a valid but completely different way of expressing how the system worked.

Even sketches that seemed similar on the surface—ones that focused on users, for instance, rather than on code or technical details—still differed in the stories they told about the product's users, and the words they used to describe it.

For example, one sales associate described the feature set they were trying to sell to clients, but used words that were unique to him. The landing page of the product was a large table, or list of customers, and they called this a *dashboard*, which sounds a bit fancier than a table.

In short, everyone defined the system based on their role, whether that required direct daily interaction with users or working in design tools or code. These experiences shaped their mental models, drawing on what they learned from their peers and the language norms in their departments—from the plain, technical language of engineering to the heightened, persuasive language of sales.

None of these mental models was wrong, as such. But the sheer variation told me that the company's idea of itself was not yet concrete.

COMMITTING TO TERMS

Once you've done some research and have a better sense of what you're trying to give shape to, you can start applying concrete terms to your concept. Applying words to an idea gives it shape, but tread carefully. Choose words that almost—but not quite—transform the idea they're trying to express.

One way of making an idea concrete is to understand where it lives—the nature of the system it's part of. By first understanding the "home system" for a new idea, it becomes easier to understand how a concept can live within it. In fact, the system defines and shapes the ideas it can house: a properly modeled system will begin to smooth the edges of an idea to give it a sense of fitness within its home.

To really go deep on understanding your system, you'll need to understand what that home system consists of, as well as how others define and think about it. You can start by simply diagramming the system or creating a content audit that lists all its features and their properties.

A diagram is a helpful beginning, but you'll need to go deeper. Two tools can help you get there: words and people. For example, you can:

- Create a text definition for your new idea—like a glossary entry—that puts it in context alongside other objects in its destined system.
- Conduct formal or informal discovery interviews. Listen to others describe the idea, and then note the mental model that surfaces in their description or definition.

Creating a home for an idea and understanding it in relation to other dimensions and objects will bring focus to the concept you're defining. Seeing how other people view a problem helps you understand what matters most about it to you and your team.

Design happens in groups, and ideas and definitions arise from the back-and-forth of group work and discussion. The tools you use to engage in those discussions can be as simple as a conversation or as crafted as a visual diagram. When it comes to defining an idea, it's okay—even necessary—to move beyond the verbal to try to visualize the concept taking shape in your mind. We all organically go back and forth between the visual and the semantic as we try to capture ideas. The moment that should give you pause is when a loose sketch of an idea quickly morphs, almost unaltered, into a detailed design. This will happen; it's inevitable. Just be sure you're not moving to high-fidelity design before the concept you're creating is really locked down. If a visual mock-up is your automatic first step in design, simply pause and consider *what* you're representing in that design, and whether your idea could be clearer. If the answer is "yes," then take a step back or dial down the fidelity of your designs to make it clear they're exploring notions, not firm details.

Visual artifacts—even when they're abstract models, not polished designs—create preconceptions about what a product might be or do. That's both their power and their limitation: all diagrams are opinionated, because they choose what to represent and thereby reduce the number of roads forward.

A good way to take a moment and pause is to talk to everyone on the design and product team—across all disciplines—about the mental models they have for certain terms you're discussing. This will help clarify how you all see the problem or product differently.

Defining your terms

Here's a common example: many products like to call themselves "platforms." (I first ran into this one while at Intercom, but have seen it crop up many times since.) If you want to use that word intentionally—as intentionally as the founders of Google thought of search—you first must define what a platform is. The word has a lot of different interpretations, including:

- The parts of a product that are exposed to the outside world: the API
- The entire product, whether it's made public or not
- A commercial agreement—the way technology and external developers link together

Each of these definitions means something a little (or a lot) different, especially to the set of external developers who might be building apps—and their livelihood—on top of a platform.

Definitions create their own truth. By defining a platform in a particular way, you begin to beg further questions about the system you're building.

If a platform is just an API, does changing the structure of that API change the nature of the platform? The answer is probably a simple yes, but when a platform's structure changes, that has a downstream effect on the developers who are building on top of it. Does the word *platform*—something that sounds like a solid foundation, a base layer—effectively describe the changeable nature of an API, which can be redesigned with huge effects on what can be built on it?

If, instead, "platform" is just another word for "product"—a big, important-sounding product—who decides what becomes a platform and what stays a product? What power does the word actually hold? Is it just a question of marketing?

Choosing a word like *platform* makes a statement about what you are making. Your audience will naturally begin to make assumptions about how this "platform" should be used. The teams building that platform, even more crucially, will start making assumptions about how they should be building it, and what it might become. And these assumptions have real-world outcomes. If a company has an implicit definition of a platform that doesn't place value on the role of outside developers, it can easily start to make decisions that don't benefit that group. The platform could get a reputation for being hard to build on and for not being engaged with one of its key audiences.

Digging into the complexity of big, undefined concepts means asking big questions about who matters most in a system, product, or platform—and about who can handle the complexity that might come with certain product decisions. Every system, and every concept within that system, requires definition and prioritization so that it can be designed more effectively.

When the user decides

The idea you're defining ultimately must be put in front of the people who will be using your product. An idea or term might make perfect sense to you as you're building it, yet still be hard for your audience to understand because of their mental models and expectations.

Expectations are a massive unexamined hurdle in product design. With every new feature or idea, you must contend with what users expect your feature to do by virtue of its name and its marketing. For example, every time you use a new email product, you trust that it is founded on the same basic concepts as every other email tool you've ever used. You'll see an inbox and folders, and your email will look something like a document that can be sent to someone.

When you search for something online, thanks to Google you now understand a simple input field to be an entire search product; it would feel odd to have to navigate into categories to narrow your search. You're far more likely to just change how you're asking a question in the search field if you don't find what you're looking for on the first try.

With a product that has many use cases or features, users have more to learn. Working on Intercom, we didn't have great success asking users what they thought our *entire* product was. The question was too big and too amorphous. There was no single concrete idea for users to respond to.

But we could still ask for and receive great user feedback for each individual feature we released. I was there when the company was developing its first chatbot, which was early enough that users didn't expect chatbots to pop up when messaging a company, as they often do today. We had to tread carefully to see how this feature would upset the conventions we'd created with Intercom's messenger, which was designed to be personal (and thus, following the received wisdom at the time, not automated).

It's not the user's job to challenge or amend their mental model to the idea of the system you have in mind. Instead, your job is to understand what expectations users already have, and then either meet them or very clearly subvert them in an arresting yet inviting way.

A bot, therefore, was a product idea that needed to be handled delicately in this context. Siri had been around for a few years, and Alexa was everywhere. There was an immediate set of assumptions:

- The bot should have a name
- It should introduce itself in the first person
- It should have a strong personality and mode of expression

We decided to do some user testing with different linguistic elements to see how users might react to the bot. Instead of simply altering the tone, I decided to take a more structural approach to interrogate the idea. We tested:

- With a name, and without one
- With a pronoun, and without one
- With a salutation like "Hi!" and without one

At first, we assumed that the more neutral, pared-back version might feel vague or even off-putting to users. How would they know what they were interacting with?

What we found was quite the opposite. Users we tested with hated the overt, named, pronoun-having bot. There was a simple, though perhaps not obvious, reason for this: they weren't aware they were entering into an automated conversation. Having encountered a messaging tool on a website, they were trying to talk to a real person. Their expectations weren't ever going to be met by a bot that made itself the center of the design idea.

We had to shift from "let's build a bot" to "let's find a way to answer questions automatically without making people mistrust this entire interface, or worry that they'll never get to a real person on the other side of it."

I wrote about this project at the time:

> *Names and identity lift the tools on the screen to a level above intuition. They [...] place it in an entirely different context to the person using it, and [that's] not always a relationship that person asks for or appreciates.* (*https://bkaprt.com/dd46/01-02*)

What I realized was that the relationship we needed to understand and design for wasn't an archetypal or personality-driven one. Instead, we were designing half of a conversation, and so we needed to understand conversation patterns—how they work, how they differ between text and speech, and what sorts of conversational tactics our little automated bot could reasonably handle.

We were creating automated conversations in a messaging app, where the human side of the conversation might reasonably not know they were entering into a conversation with a bot. This was the first distinctive detail of our concept. We had to let the user know the context, without it taking over or putting them off.

The recent advances in large language models like ChatGPT have the potential to change what bots are capable of—but I suspect user expectations of them will be slower to change. While a bot's responses may be more fluent, it still has to deliver on the same purpose: to help people get specific jobs done, quickly and conversationally.

HOW TO STAY TUNED IN

When we design digital products, ideas and concepts are staring at us daily. Each navigation label that you see on a screen represents a concept, but that doesn't mean those concepts are all road tested and well understood. Understanding the existing concepts and definitions in a product by conducting a research study or creating a glossary is a great first step toward challenging your own assumptions about what things mean. This work can uncover gaps between your mental models and those of your teammates, and will provide a baseline understanding of your concept so that when new ideas emerge that change or challenge it, you'll be better equipped to examine your own assumptions, break down the concept again, and make it more sustainable and useful.

But the journey doesn't stop there. Let's return to the idea of the bot. Now, for me, the ideal computer interaction has always been the one presented by the starship computer from TV's *Star Trek*, especially during the show's *The Next Generation* era. The computer didn't have a name; it was referred to and interacted with simply as "Computer." It answered questions, and while it had a gendered (feminine) voice, its personality wasn't foregrounded either in the story or in the short interactions characters had with it. That idea was powerful to me: an invisible, practical technology that supported humans without distracting them.

These real-world comparisons might seem removed from our design decisions, but they can become a vital way of distinguishing between a promising idea and a shaky one. Ideas don't exist in a vacuum. The frameworks we use to understand technology are based on the ideas and expectations we all bring from the real world. By digging into these mental models in ourselves, our teams, and our users, we can make our real-world ideas crisper and more clearly defined.

2 MAKING METAPHORS

Most of us think of metaphor as something poetic or ornate, a decorative flourish of communication rather than an essential tool. But we can't speak to one another without using metaphor. I remember my first reading of *Metaphors We Live By*, by George Lakoff and Mark Johnson. In it, Lakoff and Johnson showed how much of our speech is peppered with comparisons and metaphors. We use them to talk about the passage of time, about growing older, about journeys and decisions. We also use physical ideas to convey abstract ideas to one another, converting sensory images into meaning more swiftly than we could without them. There is very little in the language we use every day that doesn't rely on allusion or image-making.

Lakoff and Johnson also analyzed how our use of metaphor shapes the ideas we have and how we communicate them. We use metaphor to be better understood, and the way we seek to be understood affects how we think.

Interface design is full of metaphors. Interfaces exist to prompt a response, to get someone to do something. They're a kind of visual argument, and metaphors speed up and simplify the ways an interface makes that argument.

Metaphor has all sorts of powerful dimensions, and using metaphors mindfully—being aware of their power—can make us better communicators. Here are just a few of the doors they unlock:

- **Metaphors bring the abstractions of software closer to life, making interfaces feel real.** Different kinds of metaphors in design can transform a good product into a great one.
- **A good metaphor focuses on a special attribute of a feature.** When you apply a metaphor, you must ask yourself which concepts are most prominent in the feature you're building.
- **Thinking in metaphors helps you think in systems.** This is because metaphor, as a tool, is all about finding relationships to, and contrasts with, other things. Understanding a system through its metaphors keeps you in conversation with that system, as well as with the world beyond it.
- **Metaphor is a great simplifier.** It asks you to deeply understand something in order to compare it to something else. (It's the rhetorical form of a simplified fraction—boiling an idea down to its simplest expression.)

TYPES OF METAPHORS

In product design, we might see metaphor pop up in discussions around naming, or perhaps around the creation of icons—anytime we need to make the concept stand out in some way. While many problems of naming *are* problems of metaphor, not all metaphors have to do with names. They can also exist in visuals and speak to how things are made.

Design metaphors show up in different contexts and formats:

- **Visual metaphors** look like something in the real world and help you understand how to interact with a tool.
- **Linguistic metaphors** create a relationship between two ideas through words alone, often through the names we give to features.

- **Structural metaphors** can help us understand how something is made or see something abstract or technical in a simpler way.

Visual metaphors

A *visual metaphor* conveys a representative relationship between an interface and a real-world object through the use of a shape, icon, or other visual element.

Almost every design pattern used in product design is a visual metaphor in some way. The role of design is to create space—a workspace where people can do things, complete tasks, or read content. All of that requires us to give the user the sense that this hard, glass screen in front of them is a real, tangible place.

One extremely common visual metaphor mimics the materials we find on an office desk: cards and paper. The impression of layering and depth we see in digital card patterns, created with borders and drop shadows, mimics an assortment of physical materials that you can lift and touch. This provides a sense of space and depth and texture to create symmetry between the digital and physical (**FIG 2.1**).

Other ubiquitous visual metaphors surface in the ways we use emoji, icons, and shapes. Emoji sometimes appear in interfaces themselves, but more typically they pop up in content, replacing words and metaphors in everyday communication and on social media. One example is the "thread" emoji, now ubiquitous on Twitter, which is a metaphor for a series of linked posts. It bridges the gap between content (because it's user-generated) and interface, since it has become so ubiquitous that it does the job of an interface cue.

In an interface itself, we rely on icons much like we rely on emoji. Both patterns rely on visual metaphors, but icons tend to be more utilitarian, direct, and long-lasting than emoji (or at least less prone to the vagaries of social media trends).

The icon of a garbage can has meant "delete" for decades, and a "pin" is commonly used to denote something a user can save in one spot. At one point, my team at Shopify debated whether a pin icon in our navigation could change what was

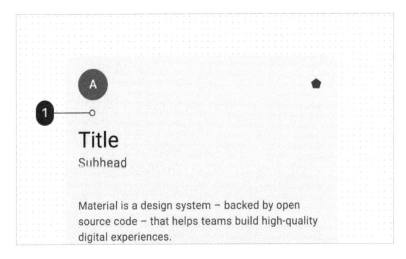

FIG 2.1: A card component from Google's Material Design (https://bkaprt.com/dd46/02-01) shows how a card can use even the subtlest line and shadow to create the illusion of depth (https://bkaprt.com/dd46/02-02).

pinned for *everyone* in the same Shopify store (**FIG 2.2**). Most actions in Shopify already worked this way. For example, if a single user fulfilled an order or updated a record, all their fellow staff members would see that change. But we felt that the pin icon was too closely associated with something that only changed *one person's view* of an experience. So we decided to stick with what felt like the industry-standard interpretation of the pin metaphor rather than attempt to make that icon work for a very different mode of interaction.

Finally, visual metaphors can take the form of simple shapes in an interface. We've mentioned cards and how they represent physical space in general, but another shape, the circle, goes even further. The circle is so commonly used to represent a person's account or avatar inside a product that it is now tightly coupled with the concept of *you*. Like a physical photo frame, a circle doesn't even need to have a photograph or drawing of a human being inside it to be seen as a stand-in for a person (**FIG 2.3**).

FIG 2.2: In Shopify's left-hand navigation menu, things that have pin icons can be controlled by individual users, while other elements appear for every user.

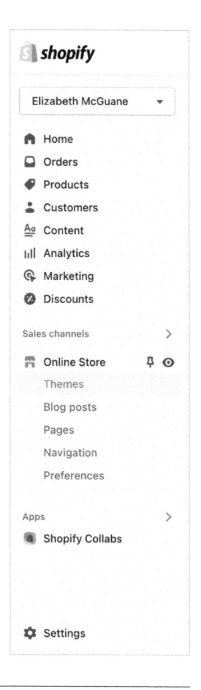

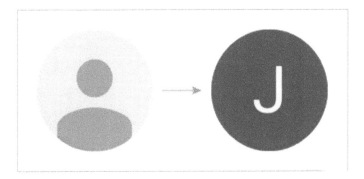

FIG 2.3: A circle can represent "person" even without many other identifying elements within it (https://bkaprt.com/dd46/02-03).

Linguistic metaphors

Some of the earliest linguistic metaphors on the internet—and in software generally—were inspired by physical ways of writing down words and saving them. An entire conceptual framework came from typing words onto pages or documents and putting them into folders (**FIG 2.4**).

Some of these metaphors have endured longer than anyone expected. Despite having been created on the fly, they continue to influence structure many decades later. Ted Nelson, the person who coined the term *hypertext*, has pointed out that describing and building software as a system of files and folders has led to a few pitfalls, one being that it relies heavily on naming for recall, because everything stored as a file must be named to be retrieved (https://bkaprt.com/dd46/02-06).

For Nelson, this metaphor limits software from being structured in other, possibly more flexible, ways. That is how fundamental metaphor is to the way we imagine and create systems. The metaphor of a file system has likely lasted so long in software design because it's such a simple yet evocative way to think about storing and sharing content.

Another metaphor that has persisted alongside the file system is the metaphor of the network, which communicates software's ability to describe ideas by grouping them together.

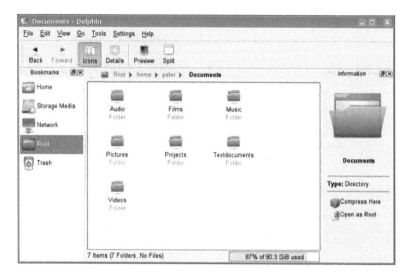

FIG 2.4: Early software applications established the metaphor of the folder system that persists today. Image by Wikipedia user Brisvegas (https://bkaprt.com/dd46/02-04) under a Creative Commons Attribution-ShareAlike 3.0 license (https://bkaprt.com/dd46/02-05), via Wikimedia Commons.

This metaphor says that the associations between objects, not just their names, is what gives them shape and definition.

Structural metaphors

Some metaphors lend themselves to reframing a design problem. They don't necessarily translate into the name we give something, or the imagery we use, the way linguistic and visual metaphors do. What they do instead is give us a new way to think about the parts of a system. They exist behind the scenes and are no less powerful for it. Their role is to help communicate an idea—not least to those actually designing the feature.

Marta Masters, a content designer at a large product company, shared an experience with me about creating a structural metaphor with her team, and it's a particularly powerful one. She and her team had been working for a few weeks on a new version of an existing product, which was a feature that let you build out your own data and analytics reports. The existing product was very much like a spreadsheet. It looked like a table, with rows and columns, and it let people interrogate data in ways familiar to advanced users of Excel.

The team knew they wanted to rethink the visual paradigm they were representing, yet they felt locked into what already existed. They just kept designing different, slightly better spreadsheets. After a three-week design sprint where engineers, designers, and product managers had collectively tried to reimagine the tool, they knew they were stuck.

Masters told me that the problem they were trying to solve wasn't just to make the product new for novelty's sake. Users often felt intimidated by what seemed like a very technical tool. But the platform—a customer-support product—required that non-technical people sometimes needed to build reports and crunch numbers. They needed to analyze things like how many support tickets had been closed in a month, and how long those conversations had taken. These were users who weren't accustomed to complex analysis, so a newer, slightly simpler spreadsheet wasn't going to cut it.

Because engineers were in the room, Masters kept hearing technical language get thrown back and forth—phrases like "data layering" were mentioned. One day, out at lunch, she thought to herself: "What else has layers and is something everyone intuitively knows how to build?"

The answer was on her plate: a sandwich. She went back to her team with a new brief: "Imagine you're trying to redesign a sandwich. What elements would you put in it? How would you make sure other people knew how to build their own sandwich?" What emerged from the brief was a little sketch that reimagined a data query as a sandwich (FIG 2.5).

This everyday metaphor didn't result in a product that literally looked like a sandwich or used sandwich-related terminology. Users never would have known that this was the metaphor underpinning the tool. But the idea allowed the team to think about the structure of their product—the elements a reporting feature required, including a visualization layer, a configuration layer, an attribution layer, and a metrics layer—in a new way.

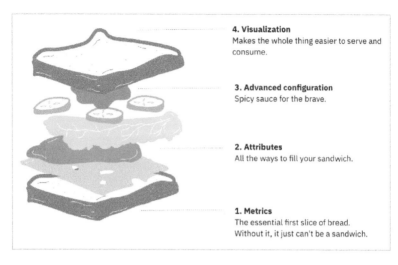

4. Visualization
Makes the whole thing easier to serve and consume.

3. Advanced configuration
Spicy sauce for the brave.

2. Attributes
All the ways to fill your sandwich.

1. Metrics
The essential first slice of bread.
Without it, it just can't be a sandwich.

FIG 2.5: The layers of a sandwich correspond to the layers of context in a data-driven report. Image courtesy of Marta Masters.

It helped them see the product in three dimensions, rather than as a two-dimensional set of rows and columns.

It was a fun visual idea, but it also had depth and a communication goal: to make the feature feel more grounded in reality, in things that could be tangibly handled. A piece of bread became the metrics; the data attributes were the ingredients that lived between the slices.

The metaphor generated new visual and interaction design ideas and broke open the design sprint. What's more, it resonated beyond the design team. Product managers referenced the sandwich idea when sharing updates with company executives. It helped them argue for new feature opportunities for the tool they were building and gave rise to a broader roadmap. The engineering team got in on it too—because the metaphor was simple, it invited open collaboration. Previously, the engineers, unfamiliar with sketching and design tools like Figma, had stayed mostly silent. The everyday nature of the metaphor also helped lower the barrier for entry to design. Likening something technical and dry to something commonplace and approachable gave the team permission to be playful.

Metaphors can be powerful simply by helping you see things differently. "It gave us permission to start somewhere else," Masters said. "We didn't have to benchmark ourselves against anything other than our imagination."

"Something amazing happens in the human brain [with a metaphor]," she told me. "If you need to bring people together into the same mental space, a metaphor is the surest way of doing it."

The sandwich metaphor was an inspired structural metaphor because it brought to life the key characteristic of what they were building: flexibility. It was fun and evocative while also telling a simple, vivid story about their product.

HOW TO SPOT A METAPHOR IN THE WILD

Before you start consciously looking for metaphors in design, it can be difficult to spot them. But once you begin, you'll see them everywhere. There are likely many metaphors buried in the experiences you use every day.

In software, metaphors often work in one of two ways by relying on:

- **Real-world, analog objects** like paper, cards, and photo frames (or even sandwiches)
- **Imaginary objects** from literature, art, and movies—robots, for example

The latter usually crop up in new technology, which can rely on metaphors from speculative fiction as a means of communicating novelty or invention. The company Meta's use of the word *metaverse* draws on fictional notions of how we might communicate with one another someday.

This can be an imprecise approach, especially if the technology being built has only a loose connection with the original fictional idea. More importantly, it risks being imprecise because it's just not as intuitive as a real-world example that most people are familiar with.

In general, metaphors work best when drawn from reality, and that's where you and your team might want to start when generating new concepts during design discovery.

Generating metaphors

In Chapter 1, we learned about using drawings or diagrams to uncover mental models of how a system works. This method can also be used to generate new metaphors. One common design sketching exercise is known as Crazy Eights. In this exercise, you and your teammates fold pieces of paper into eight sections, set your timer for eight minutes, and try to quickly sketch eight ideas.

Crazy Eights is usually used to sketch interface ideas, but it can also be used to generate metaphors. To do this, try following this set of prompts:

- What would this feature look like in the real world, not on a screen? What materials would it be made of?
- Is there anything in the real world that reminds you of this feature?
- How should this feature make you feel?

The aim is to answer questions that focus less on a user journey, problem domain, or specific interface and instead ask you to riff and create associations. This should generate ideas that feel very far removed from your current concept—and it might feel uncomfortable at first! Push through it and lean into the playfulness this type of exploration offers. You'll have plenty of chances later on to dig into *why* you're building what you're building. This exercise helps you imagine *the feelings and associations* connected with what you're building, creating new directions to explore.

Avoid overreaching

Because metaphor is so pervasive, we can use it to make connections between ideas without realizing it—and can sometimes create relationships that are misleading or unhelpful.

A weak metaphor is a dangerous thing. By "weak," I mean metaphors that imply loose or unclear connections between things, or that borrow from an established concept to create unfounded trust in something new or untested. Such metaphors usually fall apart under close scrutiny. One example is the richly immersive metaphor of the Metaverse, which paints a loftier (and more densely populated) picture than virtual reality platforms have so far achieved. A subtler and more deceptive example is the metaphor of the "wallet" in cryptocurrency, which creates an aura of simplicity, security, and dependability that softens the real risks of that technology.

Metaphors can be dangerous simply because ideas are powerful, especially in the nebulous space of software. When an idea is described in software, it is literally created and made real. A metaphor becomes the scaffolding products are built on, generating spaces that don't exist until they are described.

To describe a space clearly enough to make it real, we need more than a loose metaphor; we need to give the space the right handle—the right *name*. We'll talk about that in Chapter 3.

EMBRACE METAPHOR

Metaphor is a form of instant storytelling, and it can play a huge role in defining a concept before you ever open a design document or think about an interface. Once you do begin to shape your design, you'll get into more sequential, literal forms of narrative. At this stage, though, what matters most is not the journey but the central theme or idea you're trying to convey. On its own, a strong metaphor or theme can instantly generate new ideas and new avenues to explore. Perhaps because it is a visual idea in linguistic form, metaphor is a uniquely powerful precursor to visual exploration. While visual exploration on its own can constrain how you think about problems, visuals that rely on new metaphors can blow your ideas wide open.

3 NAMING THE DAMN THING

COMING UP WITH A NAME for an idea seems like it should be a simple task. After all, each one of us was named at birth. Things we use every day have names. We name our pets, and sometimes we name our cars. A name is usually a single word, which should be the easiest thing in the world to bestow. You just think of a noun, apply it to something, and then watch that thing begin to embody the name, so that you can't imagine it being called anything else.

In the realm of software, however, naming has a quiet reputation for slipperiness and difficulty. It's become something of a cliche that *naming is one of the hardest problems in computer science.* (The actual quote, attributed to a Netscape engineer named Phil Karlton by his colleague Martin Fowler, says that naming is one of two "hard problems," the other being cache invalidation, which I'm maybe not enough of an engineer to truly understand (https://bkaprt.com/dd46/03-01).

What makes it hard—and really, I don't believe it is hard, just misunderstood and rushed through—is the focus required to create a name that doesn't just sound good, but also fits within a system and can evolve with a product.

As we explore how names are constructed, their powerful role in the very foundations of software becomes more and more evident. That power needn't be something we struggle with; we can approach naming during product design in a way that enriches and enlivens—rather than interrupts—the creative process.

HOW NAMES WORK

A name is a word that expresses both an idea (what something is) and a function (what something does).

A good name is also an intuitive name: one that immediately evokes what the concept is. But moving from even a well-defined concept toward a single word that expresses that concept intuitively is a tall order.

In a product sense, names are nouns that represent collections of tools and associated actions. Sometimes a name will be converted directly into an action word. For example, the primary noun of Twitter is the "tweet," which is also the verb used to describe it. The distance between noun and verb isn't always this short (or is nonexistent), but because interfaces are primarily interactive, a noun and its associated actions never live very far apart. This means that a well-named product is directly connected to the use of that product—how it can be interacted with. What isn't named well can't be as easily used.

Product names can take a few different forms:

- **Sometimes names are abstract nouns.** Facebook and Google are examples of this, as their utility is almost completely abstracted (bar the fact that there are faces in Facebook and the search results in Google may reach very high numbers).
- **Sometimes names describe action or utility.** Shopify is quite literally a product that allows anyone to open an online shop.
- **And sometimes names are a metaphor.** Twitter is so named because of the incomprehensible sounds of birds chattering. (This metaphor has not only become painfully apt, but also insulting to birds.)

The last example in the list is probably the hardest to do well, especially at the feature level rather than at the brand level. As we explored in Chapter 2, a strong metaphor—like a sandwich, when talking about data—can be a useful tool for sharing and breaking down concepts and ideas. When it comes to a name, the metaphor is often far more subtle, and must stand alone rather than being supported by definitions and diagrams.

As soon as a name becomes established—whether it's in the real world or in a product or system—it begins to evolve. Its very success leads it toward change. Sometimes this happens through a change in the way the name is used. As with the "tweet/tweet" (noun/verb) example, what starts out as a noun doesn't stay a noun. If it's successful, it can often be "verbed." This "verbing" can pull the metaphor away from its origins and make it more nuanced and flexible. For example, the noun *crane* describes a kind of bird with a long neck; used as a metaphor, the word refers to a construction machine that has a long neck. We also use the noun as a verb: the act of "craning" evokes the long, slender neck of the bird, but we often use "craning" to describe a kind of curious, even nosy, kind of looking (similar to "rubbernecking"). With each of these transformations, we think less about the origin of the word—the bird—and more about the actions it's associated with. Yet the verb instantly makes sense to us because of its metaphorical origin.

Similarly, if a feature name has a strong association with a root metaphor (the way "tweet" evokes a short "chirp" of communication), then any transformation we make to that name—turning it into a verb, applying it to different contexts—will make intuitive sense to those who hear it.

Some real-world names also work intuitively, not because of metaphor but because of *synecdoche:* when the name for something specific becomes the handle for something generic, and this specific name becomes widely adopted. These are often brand names that become everyday terms for items like Kleenex, which is commonly substituted in the US for *tissue*; or Hoover, which, in other English-speaking countries, is synonymous with *vacuum cleaner*. Those transitions happen gradually, as a product gains traction and becomes synonymous with the use case it serves.

Everyday names and system names

In most cases, everyday names and new ideas appear and spread at a relatively slow pace, though perhaps global media and the internet help them spread faster than in the past. With software, however, the sheer velocity at which products are shipped means that new names are constantly created—and by all sorts of people with different skill sets and goals. Product designers have to come up with new labels for things nearly every time they create a feature. That means considering new ideas, making the utility of those ideas apparent, and even generating new metaphors.

Often, those creating these names aren't specialists in language and aren't thinking about the roots of words. A Shopify colleague of mine, content designer Quentin Dietrich, told me about a framework he has for thinking and talking with his colleagues about the different ways language works. He calls it *everyday language versus system language.*

EVERYDAY LANGUAGE	SYSTEMS LANGUAGE
• Is derived from its use and context • Shifts over time • Can function in different ways • Is flexible and can mean different things	• Is derived from the system • Is relatively fixed over time • Usually functions in one way • Has limited flexibility and should mean only one thing

A similar model could easily be applied to everyday names and system names.

EVERYDAY NAMES	SYSTEM NAMES
• Are derived from shared associations and metaphors • Can be understood without deeply interrogating their metaphor • Are lexible and often borrowed to apply to other things	• Are consciously created and fixed • Their meaning changes when the underlying system changes • Have limited flexibility and should mean only one thing

FIG 3.1: Clippy is the early automated bot that all bots are unfairly measured against.

It is to the detriment of the system if a name within that system is used to describe more than one thing—the kind of messy free association that makes everyday language so vibrant is a sign of a system problem in any designed taxonomy.

Let's have a look at how that framework applies to software and, especially, to the product design process.

System names and software

Names are crucial in part because of the way the internet has been built. As we discussed in Chapter 1, the internet's founding concepts and foundational architecture are articulated around a system of files and folders. Those files and folders need to have names on them to be retrieved and used.

System names are hard not only because of what they imply, but also often because of what they imply accidentally. A good example is the name *chatbot*. It implies an automated tool that can talk to an end user. But early on, some chatbots leaned heavily on the word *chat* and created experiences that were almost intrusively chatty, invoking ridicule not experienced since the days of Microsoft's Clippy (FIG 3.1). A capability or function of the tool had become a slightly negative aspect of how it was perceived.

So, system names imply function, and they also imply certain attributes. Because of that, a system name chosen for a product imposes entirely conceptual, but still very strong, limits on what users, developers, and designers think that product can do.

HOW TO MAKE A NAME

A handle is essential for communicating an idea from one person to another. This is why conceptual work often hinges on and focuses on the name we choose: a name is the primary tool teams need to collaborate on an idea. Often, design and product teams will skip over the early, rougher stages of conceptual work—the idea and the metaphors that bring it to life—and go straight to the name.

This can be an unexpectedly tricky place to start, though it might feel very objective and solid. To leave space in design for possibility, a team can approach naming differently at each stage of the design process:

- **Starting out:** When starting design exploration, the attitude toward names should be flexible and open. Teams working on a project need names to understand ideas together, but keeping names loose at this point has benefits later.
- **Framing the problem:** As the design evolves, the choice of a name will help frame the problem. This is part of the connecting process; as the concept evolves, its working name and the ideas it represents will need clear, simple framing. Look for names to become simpler, and for ways to make decisions about the tone and inspiration for your name.
- **Fitting it to the system:** The name will start to appear in the interface itself, in labels on navigation, in buttons and titles on pages, but it will also take its place alongside other features, and the name you choose will help it fit well—or not—with other products in a system.

- **Taking it to market:** Pitching a product and taking it to market require an outward focus on naming and the ways the name will land with its audience.

A name must remain malleable enough to be challenged at each stage of the process; different lights will be cast on the name as it moves through these dimensions.

Starting out

Words are a lever for understanding the present and imagining the future. What's magical about focusing on defining concepts before naming them is that when you unlock meaning, you unlock deeper understanding. A design team gains a shared sense of the world they're building, and that's powerful.

All early conceptual work is a vulnerable act. It's the point in the design process when a team has figured out the smallest part of their problem space. That vulnerability can make us feel eager to reach toward the shores of certainty. And naming a thing can make it feel solid, for sure. At the same time, locking into a name too early can lead to trickiness, particularly if the concept evolves past that early name.

It's important to remember that the name is always the loose cap that holds in an idea: it's the idea that needs to be understood. So while your concept is percolating, you can look for ways to keep the naming process flexible.

Debating a loose set of names and descriptions in a name brainstorming workshop can invite participants to play with different ways of framing a concept. In a workshop context, proceed with the understanding that you're trying to create different ways of seeing the problem, rather than trying to establish the final go-to-market name. You might experiment with using a name that's never going to see the light of day. Or you might want to avoid single-word names and instead apply a longer phrase to describe the concept. Something short and memorable, but not too "nouny."

Some of the research and drawing exercises outlined in Chapter 1 are great places to start, but you can also try these:

- **Write a press release:** Marketing exercises can quickly clarify how a name will feel in the real world. Try writing a fake landing page, press release, or other marketing tool. A fun exercise is to imagine advertising your product on the front and back of a cereal box—to describe the product in simple terms. Focusing on its key selling points and simple language can break you out of a tendency to use insider jargon or technical language, a trap we all fall into.
- **Imagine the future:** Draw or write out an imaginary roadmap for your feature, and think about how its name or description might change as it evolves. Think of a name that could be used at launch, in two years, or in ten years.

These approaches will help you to think about two things: how quickly a name can be understood, and how it needs to evolve. Every name has a life span, and digital products are very prone to change that transforms what they are. Imagining the future of your product, even if it's not the precise future that will actually unfold, helps you ask important questions:

- Does the name need to describe the product as it is today?
- Does the name need to describe what the product might grow into?

These naming exercises can build a collective sense of perspective while giving the concept time to find its feet.

Framing the name

Once a concept has started to take shape, you'll need to factor in more heavy-hitting market and system research, bringing in materials that go beyond your initial imagination and brainstorming.

First, it's worth thinking about the nature of the concept you're naming. Some concepts are foundational and will inform other parts of your system. They'll need to have other names that connect with them in meaningful ways. Other features can sit lightly on top of your system and will have fewer dependencies. You can place your concept on an axis that considers its

	Foundational concept	Surface-level concept
Utilitarian name	Major concepts in your product need utilitarian names, because they interact with so many parts of your product.	Many small features will get basic, utilitarian names that simply describe what they do.
Branded name	Your biggest product launches might get brand names.	Some small features might get brand names, but much more rarely

FIG 3.2: Figure out what role a name fits into based on its prominence in your architecture and how loudly it should be communicated.

role in your system, and its market importance (**FIG 3.2**). Its role might be foundational, so that the name informs or appears in multiple places and has an influence on other features. Think of something as essential as the name "post" in most blogging and social media products. This is a foundational name that will persist for a long time. Or the name might be surface-level, describing a smaller feature set, and that perhaps makes it a bit more transient. Then the market importance of the name will influence whether you need to embellish it with the name of your company, or whether it stands on its own as a utility.

(Imagine if Facebook had named a foundational utilitarian feature like a post on its news feed a "Facebook News Feed Post." It's a mouthful!)

Deciding whether a name should be branded as a standalone product is a business or marketing choice, one centered around how prominent the business wants the feature to be and how much they want to stake a kind of ownership over it. But it's also a choice that affects the user experience. If a feature is foundational, you may not want to saddle it with a lengthy brand name that will need to be used over and over again in your documentation and interface. You might also want to choose a name that's deliberately not branded or differentiated, because it'll have competitors out in the wild that you'll want customers to be able to compare it to. Giving it an individualized or branded name might get in the way of that useful comparison.

Branding and utility

I spoke with Candi Williams, head of content design at the dating app Bumble, about how her content design team has approached naming in their product. Bumble has such a strong brand-forward approach, with its metaphor-rich name and mixture of brand-led marketing features and utilitarian features. She said there is often a tension between the two types of names, and her aim has been to make sure new features are easily recognizable.

Williams found that colleagues moved too swiftly to naming and bee-associated terms, without framing the concept they were designing for first. Often the concept wasn't clear, and her team was looking for a name when they weren't quite sure what they should be naming.

Her content design team created naming guidelines for a range of branded and unbranded names used across Bumble, from the evocative (like *Bumble* itself) to the descriptive (like *Swipe*).

These guidelines for whether things needed to be branded or not helped her team understand when to bring in bee concepts and when to be pragmatic. If a name is going to appear as a field label, for example, they lean on a utilitarian word that simply describes the feature. Think of the word *swipe*, which describes the action the user needs to take. In ubiquitous features, descriptiveness and clarity are more important than being part of a brand theme (bees and honey, in Bumble's case). Williams said she also advises designers to lean more on descriptive names than branded ones because Bumble is fundamentally a mobile experience, so they are dealing with an interface with minimal space.

Branded and evocative names, then, should be used judiciously so they stand out all the more. The brand names that end up resonating with people are often surprising. As a metaphor, the word *bumble* and the dating association with bees is slightly unexpected in its own right, as Williams pointed out to me.

Research approaches

I have been in many a naming brainstorm session (a *namestorm*, if you will) that relied on very little research at all. Imagine groups of people furiously looking up names in their dictionaries, exploring unexpected connotations and dusty etymology. The selection of a name can often feel very subjective and intuitive.

As we've said, names are an emotional and subjective lens on a product and can immediately start to carry weight. Your first step is to do some idea exploration—examining mental models, coming up with new metaphors—to make sure you and your team are aligned on what you're naming.

- **Market research:** Do some market research to see what terms are used elsewhere. What are products like yours called? What products are using names you've thought of? Are they actually doing the same thing you want to do?
- **Language audits:** Do an audit of all the words in your own system language. Are there names you've already used in the past that this name echoes? How much of an overlap is there? Maintaining a "burn list" of names helps with this. New people will join your company and will think of names

you've already thought of. Do them a favor and have a public glossary of names ready for them to review.

- **Product capability audits:** Compare your current and planned products and their capabilities with the names you use for them. How does the name you're considering fit within the products you already have and what they do?
- **User listening studies:** Conduct listening studies to see how your customers use a given term. Do they echo what they see in the UI, or do they replace your chosen term with their own? If you have an abundance of time, do some detailed interviews to find out what their mental models are for the space you're designing for. If time or other resources are scarce, look at social media messages, support conversations, or any other material created by your customers.

If you start with a name without doing the work of definition, you might find yourself mired in long debates.

Fitting a name to the system

Let's say you've come up with the most apt metaphor specifically for your product, and you've grounded it in a common understanding of what your team intended to build and what your audience wanted. Once you've accomplished that, you must move that concept into the right spot in your product. It needs to live and feel comfortable alongside other parts of the system.

This gap between an idea and its expression comes with some pitfalls. We can fall in love with how something sounds without fully digging into how it will be heard by others. We might spend hours in meetings arguing over the name for an idea rather than aligning on the idea itself. And often, as we've already discussed, when we argue about a name, we might also be misaligned on the concept.

To get ahead of those arguments, it helps to focus on how your name will be understood rather than relying on your own interpretation of words. Words are wonderfully messy, and not at all objective. If you're choosing a name, the best way to bring clarity is not to look for absolute meaning but instead to focus on your customers—how do *they* understand the word? How are they likely to respond to it? How are you framing the word? Are you placing this name in the story of your product in a way that makes sense?

To answer those questions, the following three lenses or approaches can help:

- **Novelty:** How standard or unique should your name be?
- **Flexibility:** Does it work well in multiple contexts?
- **Memorability:** Is it easy to recall?

These questions are vital when exploring a name because they prevent us from responding to names out of bias, familiarity, and emotion. Let's look at what these questions can uncover.

Novelty

Weighing novelty is a matter of deciding what value lies in your name standing out from the crowd. On the surface, that might seem like an absolute good. Don't things that stand out get noticed? But being different, at least when it comes to naming digital products, can make it harder to compare your feature with others in the market. It can also make it harder for users to understand what your feature *does*, especially if many other platforms use a standard name for it.

Standardization is a solid starting point for most products, because so many of the features we create are not genuinely new. It makes sense to start with the words you're confident your users know. Familiarity is a huge asset for adoption.

However, you must make sure that the thing you're building is truly the same as other popular products—that it's a match in terms of its capabilities or feature set. Sometimes a similarly named feature can be a *false friend*, meaning that it might share a name but diverge noticeably from its competitors in the market. When the same term is used for things that don't share capabilities, it can hem in the flexibility of what's being built. It can prevent a product from evolving as easily and swiftly as it should, simply because other products with that name don't share a given capability.

FIG 3.3: On the Intercom messaging platform, this feature helped the user rate a single conversation in the moment, rather than rating the entire Intercom brand.

For example, I once helped design a feature that appeared at the end of a support conversation in a messaging interface. There was considerable argument that we should call this feature "NPS," which stands for "Net Promoter Score." The problem was that this feature wasn't measuring NPS by any stretch of the imagination.

NPS asks people whether they would recommend a brand or a service overall, while the feature we had designed was a simple feedback form asking if a specific support interaction went well (**FIG 3.3**). I argued in favor of a specific name that spoke to what the tool did: "conversation rating." This became the final feature name of the product—a utilitarian, does-what-it-says-on-the-tin name that didn't overpromise.

Though the conversation rating name won out, it was not before several tough conversations about whether the feature could compete in the market with NPS tools. NPS tools were popular and attractive to people who might have bought our product. But it wasn't what we'd built.

Choosing an industry-standard term used elsewhere in your market over a new and unique term might seem like an easy choice to make. Standardization brings vast, immediate benefits: familiarity, findability and ranking, and immediate ease of use. In a world driven by search engines, true novelty often isn't worth the trouble.

Uniqueness is valuable, though, when a product is genuinely innovative. In those situations, it's fascinating how quickly a unique name can become memorable and even ubiquitous. For example, think about how quickly the name "Google" came to be associated with search, mutating into a verb and almost completely replacing the utilitarian word that describes it.

A genuinely new product with a new name can succeed if it brings something unexpected to the table, provided people also quickly understand what it can do. A new name should still be simple, evocative, and intuitive. The goal is to *make the new familiar, and the familiar new*.

Flexibility

Understanding whether a name will work means placing it in contexts that go beyond the interface being designed. A name needs to have not only the flexibility to travel well, but also a kind of *mutability*—the capacity to change its shape in different contexts.

You can test the flexibility and transformability of your name by asking a few different questions, and by taking it out of its designed context as much as possible:

- Does it flex to different levels of complexity—as a call to action, in a text link, or in combination with other words?
- Does it mutate from a noun to a verb, while keeping its origins clear?
- Does it work in different locations? Can it be described in a help document, or in a conversation with someone, and not lose its meaning?

To answer the first question, you'll need to add the name to your user flows—to your product itself. Working with a content designer or without one, you can see how a name inhabits the interface at different volumes.

Your name is most often going to need to mutate from noun to verb when you're writing about your feature in a help document or press release. By writing snippets of text that might be included in those documents, you can quickly see how well it stands up outside the interface itself.

Last, you can also try speaking the name aloud, because your support and sales teams will need to refer to it without visual aids. This is a great way to determine clarity: take away every other design element, and you'll soon see if a name can support its own weight.

Memorability

Memorability—how easily a product name can be recalled—is the most important but also the most ephemeral aspect of naming. It asks whether a name feels familiar. That's a difficult thing to establish at the outset, and a qualitative idea that's hard to measure outright. Still, a couple of questions can serve as early detection methods for whether a name is memorable or not:

- Does it fit with the terms it sits beside?
- Do users organically start mirroring it in their language once it's introduced, or are they always stumped when they try to remember what "that thing" is called?

Recall is a struggle, not just for novel concepts and names, but old ones too. Old concepts can be equally hard to recall if their name doesn't fit the mental model users hold in their heads. For example, people sometimes use different names for parts of a system, even when it's a long-standing part. This might be as simple as users referring to the homepage of your product as a *dashboard* even when it doesn't use dashboard-like patterns, such as visualizations of metrics or data. You might call your homepage a *feed* and have a very different product strategy in mind for it. That difference can be a symptom of a deeper misalignment with your audience, a sign that they aren't quite tuned in to your product's essential ideas.

Even when the difference is mild and not immediately problematic, it's still a difference that creates confusion. Anytime you want to direct users to a part of the product on a support call or in a help doc, you'll need to define which part of the system you're talking about, since you can't rely on a common vernacular.

Recall is also at the root of the internet's architecture. As we've discussed, any folder and file structure you create in building software—the parts of your navigation, the name of a page or document—must have a name so that it can be retrieved and referenced. Names are like windows on every part of software, and recall and retrieval are the ways we know which window to look through.

Taking a name to market

Naming is part of the design process and the marketing process. Positioning a product to go to market requires that it has a clear underlying concept that *can* be positioned. You want to make sure your product's framing doesn't fall apart when it's time to go to market. Putting an ill-conceived product through the marketing sausage-maker will, for sure, force it to reckon with its ambiguities—but ambiguity isn't just a positioning problem: it's a conceptual one. It means the product idea and its design have not been well articulated.

When I spoke with Candi Williams of Bumble, she told me her team often decides against choosing evocative or ambiguous names if marketing isn't going to be heavily involved in the process. A great deal of specialized work is involved in making sure an evocative brand name (like "Bumble" itself) will land with people, even when they're not looking at the interface. A product and content designer's job is to make sure the product interface is coherent and intuitive. Names divorced from that context have a lot more weight to carry.

Without marketing's help to dream up something new, many teams rely on familiar names from other products. We are inclined to borrow familiar names partly because naming is a design exercise that doesn't always have a clear owner, especially if there's no content designer or product marketer on board. I've often observed people showing doubt and vulnerability during the naming phase, even when they have a content background. There are so many open questions. Should you aim for a pragmatic name? An entirely new brand? Are you willing to put yourself on the line for something novel? New names gain attention inside a large company—it's like putting a sticker on your product that says, "Notice me!"

Many teams only have clear naming rules for certain high-level parts of a product—when to use branded names, when to use industry standards, when to be utilitarian—and leave many individual naming decisions up to individuals. That means only some concepts get the benefit of branding exercises that think deeply about a name and how it will be understood. And that means the teams building out the rest of the product tend to mimic what they see around them, rather than carry out in-depth naming exercises of their own.

With a little bit of focus on what's going on beneath a name, it's possible to be more strategic about the names you choose.

Who should be involved?

If naming exercises are formalized, the question of ownership and process can become a sticking point. Many stakeholders will have opinions about the right name to choose.

Because naming is such a nuanced exercise with so many dimensions, I believe it's in the safest hands when it's owned by someone with a focus on language: a content designer, a taxonomist, or an information architect. These folks can and should work closely with product and marketing teams to make sure the name fits business needs, but they'll also make sure it works as a system element.

Marketing and branding have a very specific lens on naming that complements the structural and product expertise that comes from content design and IA. Also, not every product will be broadly publicized—some features are launched and discovered organically, and so may not benefit from detailed marketing attention.

Content designers who do own the naming process—as they do at Bumble—should of course involve others in their explorations and explain their choices with a clear rationale that explains *why* they've chosen a name that is either evocative or descriptive, foundational or surface-level, branded or utilitarian.

Naming trends

We've already talked about the difference between everyday and system language, and how much they influence each other. And increasingly, everyday language is itself inspired by system language.

In the Web 1.0 era, and again in the early 2010s, many internet and product companies incorporated system language into their registered business names. Following a tech giant's name with a ".com" was common. At Intercom, the company tried to avoid being called "Intercom.io"—its original URL—but only saw that tendency among its users evolve when it changed its address to "Intercom.com."

This influence is present on social platforms in the current era, but the influence of systems on the everyday is more complex than ever. Now, the pervasive influence of algorithms impacts how people communicate online. On TikTok, users often use different terminology and their own kind of rhyming slang to communicate with one another in a way algorithms won't pick up on, since they feel TikTok's algorithms will downvote content based on a set of words, even if those words are captured without context. According to the *Washington Post*:

> *Algospeak refers to code words or turns of phrase users have adopted in an effort to create a brand-safe lexicon that will avoid getting their posts removed or down-ranked by content moderation systems. For instance, in many online videos, it's common to say "unalive" rather than "dead."* (https://bkaprt. com/dd46/03-02)

This is a new form of systems language that is *also* everyday language to those who use it. Language changes driven by internet vernacular have been happening for decades, a phenomenon that Gretchen McCullough has written about extensively in her excellent book *Because Internet: Understanding the New Rules of Language* (https://bkaprt.com/dd46/03-03).

These patterns in online speech are formed by the platforms we create, and they will very likely start getting knitted back into the systems that created them—not just in the language users create to communicate, but in the interface language present in many products, and eventually in feature or product names themselves. Systems vocabulary is always influenced by real-world speech, and now it has begun to be recursively influenced by itself.

WHEN NAMES CHANGE

Naming is where the concept usually emerges in a design project, simply because there needs to be a handle for an idea to communicate it to someone else and collaborate on it. We often skip over the stages of conceptual clarity we've already described—the idea and its many possible metaphors.

What becomes tricky is when we get locked into a name too early and then worry we're making a mistake if we change it. You might think that system names for features and products, being primarily functional, should be more fixed and stable than esoteric user language. If names in systems evolve at all, they should evolve in a less fickle, more serious way than social language does.

In systems, names become elastic when they're applied to different use cases and used to mean more than one thing. But even without that, any word's meaning in a system—whether it's expressed internally as a concept, is present in code, or is visible in a user interface—can change over time.

New name, same product?

Google has often played fast and loose with its approach to naming its products. It once had a social network called Circles, which evolved into Google+, which after several years quietly evolved into Currents, a social network for enterprise custom-

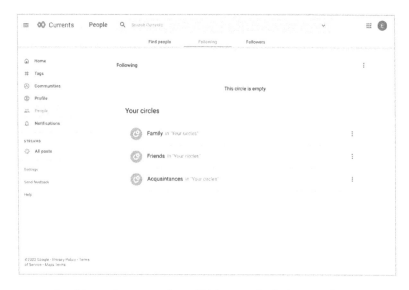

FIG 3.4: Google's new Currents product, which is targeted at businesses and teams, contains echoes of the Circles product, which focused on friends and family connections.

ers. To complicate matters, the product named Currents retained design elements—the customer-oriented "Circles" concept—from its precursor (**FIG 3.4**). Was it a new product, or just a new name? Google appears to constantly update its nomenclature, especially around social and news-oriented features. Currents became Google Play Newsstand, which then became Google News; Currents also has a relationship with Google Chat, which is now becoming "Spaces." It can be hard to gauge when these new names represent a genuinely new idea and product set, and when they're an exercise in rebranding.

When this type of change happens, it can feel like whiplash to the users of these products, who are forced to deduce whether the underlying product goal has changed, or just the name. Names are handles for things, and when those handles change shape, the nature of what they refer to starts to feel vague, making it hard to find the edges of what makes the product distinct.

To some degree, the approach Google has taken is justified. It's just words doing what words do: they try to represent an evolution of a concept. When it's done many times over, though, users start to doubt whether there's any real novelty in a feature given a new name; instead, they might start to see rebranding exercises as just that—here is the new thing, same as the old thing. Be sure your new name, then, is justified and feels distinct from previous iterations.

New names that evolve the feature

When name changes are justified—when a feature iteration is truly a leap forward—a new name can still be tough to land. This can be because of the user's comfort level with language flexibility. Many users might feel that names should be fixed in a system and that nothing should change, even though reality demands a change. In many cases, the evolution of words in a system is a good thing, and—within reason, and properly managed—can be a sign of a healthy, growing product ecosystem. But the best way to generate acceptance for that change is to go straight to your users' language and see what *they* would choose to call your feature.

Some friends and former colleagues of mine created a startup to help product teams organize their tools and documents online. They had in mind a feature they named "Projects." It was a way for people to group pages together—different Google documents or material from various tools. They referred to the feature as "Projects" from the start, even mentioning it in the slide deck they used to raise venture capital.

Then, there came a time when they needed to think of the feature in a new way—and this happened partly because of the realization that their user base wasn't quite what they'd thought it was. The startup team's perception was that their product was designed for product teams very much like theirs. When they spoke to their users about the "Projects" feature, it became obvious that the name prompted different thoughts in their users' minds than they had expected.

Project, it turns out, is seen as a heavy, loaded term. A project is *work*, and it requires certain things to function (like collaborators, a timeline, and milestones). The team realized that users thought the feature was going to require lots of configuration to set up and manage. They heard users say things like, "I don't really know what I should do [with this feature]. Should I just make it for company projects, or should I be doing it for my own work?" That wasn't the team's vision for the feature at all.

After much soul-searching, the team went back to that reliable, utilitarian software concept: the folder. As a name, *Folders* felt much more lightweight and fit better with people's mental model for easy organization of their work.

Another interesting thing happened after the team made the switch to "Folders." Their users changed how they used the feature. Unexpectedly, they began to use it for personal projects that required very little plan or structure to spin up, rather than just using it for work projects. While this wasn't a use case the team had aimed for, it opened up some new possibilities for them to consider—about what their product could do, and even whom it was for.

This meant leaving behind some possible futures they'd dreamed of. "Projects" had fit well conceptually with other features they had planned to ship, like status updates or collaboration features. Yet they realized it wasn't the right foundation for their customer base. If they lost customers at a crucial time in their growth, they'd lose their chance to build many of those other planned features.

The change was worth the cost. To correspond with the uptick in personal project use, the team started designing interaction elements like drag and drop, which more closely matched the folder concept. It was a simple metaphor with very different powers of suggestion than their original name.

There are no perfect choices when it comes to finding a name, but names are powerful and can shape the future of a product—even a company's very *self-definition* in its early days. When a foundational object name is changed, it can change the way a company thinks about the jobs it does and the market it serves. A taxonomy is a powerful tool in a small startup. It can and should be reviewed as both product and company grow, especially as names and ideas become entrenched. Never be afraid of going to the source—your users—for revelation and validation about your taxonomy. As this company found, if a name is better for the users, it's better for the product—and the company.

Names and communities

There are also times when a name change isn't required. One example is the concept of a *developer environment*. There really isn't another name for the type of tool it describes. It is very much a standardized name. Now, an industry-standard name is a great thing to be able to lean on, but it sometimes covers up a lack of consensus about meaning.

A developer environment is ostensibly a space for developers to work: a place for them to ship code. They might be building an app that's going to work with another product, and they need a place to publish that app so it can be used with the product it's designed for. Every product that calls itself a platform—that allows third parties to build on and extend their software—likely has a developer environment in some form.

But that doesn't mean it's perfectly understood. A colleague of mine was working on building a developer environment for Shopify. The developers they were designing for needed two things from this new feature: a staging environment to work on and test their app, and a production environment from which to ship it.

As part of the design process, they talked to developers inside the company who were familiar with Shopify, and to developers outside the company who might use the feature when it was done. What they found was that these communities of developers did not share a unified definition of what a developer environment should contain. There were many strong opinions, but no obvious industry standard.

So while the term *environment* was used by everyone, the hazy nature of what that word could contain meant there wasn't a clear path for them to follow. They were constantly getting pushback about the concept and what it could do. Some platforms allowed users to create multiple environments that linked together, which, to some developers, violated an assumed rule that environments should function independently—even though creating linked environments was convenient for developers. Almost any combination of different options seemed viable, depending on which developer they spoke to. And along with all this variation, there were very strong assumptions that each person had the so-called "correct" mental model.

The developer community is vocal but also a little bit opaque to outsiders—even to the designers working with them. The designers on the team were very aware of the discomfort of challenging such a strong community on its language.

What worked for this design team was simply being transparent. The team showed developers how much their ideas varied, visualizing all the different possible mental models they had heard about (a lot like the Intercom system drawings discussed in Chapter 1).

What this demonstrated was that, though the name was standard and the tools weren't, there was *enough* similarity in their *output* to accommodate the difference. The result of the environment was always a published piece of software, so the different approaches to getting there didn't throw developers off. My colleague commented that developers seemed to know what they needed when they saw it; also, they didn't seem to remember a lot of the variation.

Sometimes, the power of a name in software is so strong that it can accommodate all sorts of odd variation in usage—just as names in everyday language can accommodate different applications. An industry standard is a powerful tool, even when it's more of a blunt instrument than a precise one. Names, after all, are a handle or a way in to an idea. Sometimes by aiming to be exact and precise, we miss what names should do before anything else: they should identify a space. In the end, the design work this team did to investigate the meaning of "developer environment" didn't result in a name change, but it did lead to a stronger, more resilient understanding of their concept and their users.

THE LABEL IS THE HANDLE

There's a common principle in product design that we should all aim to have: *strong ideas, weakly held*. This is never truer than when it comes to naming. Product names evolve. In fact, challenging a name throughout the design process is a healthy sign. It shows a willingness to draw focus back to the *meaning* behind the name that was originally selected, rather than attaching the product to a particular handle just because it's memorable.

The process of naming benefits from an array of inputs— from technical folks, from marketers, from executives—yet it lives or dies by having one clear owner who can do the work of understanding all the potential pitfalls a certain name might have. It is not an easy process, but it is an enlightening one. Because a name, perhaps more than anything else, is the first and most visible introduction to the story of a product.

4

IDEAS, JOURNEYS, AND STORIES

DESIGN IDEAS DO NOT BECOME fully realized simply by choosing the right metaphors and names to define them. To go further, we need to understand these ideas in different contexts—to see them as part of a product's story.

This means understanding your idea as part of an overall narrative, and seeing where it creates new branches in that narrative. Capturing ideas through this lens brings them into sharper focus and helps refine them as they move down the road toward execution.

Narrative is a massive topic that would take an entirely different book to unpack. When you're thinking about how it might show up in a product, remember that narrative is all about perspective. Think of stories as a way of bringing ideas to life by relating them to other ideas. So when translating story to product, the nugget you're looking for is relationship. You're looking for things that are similar and things that contrast with one another. By finding those relationships, you'll find elements of the narrative your product is—perhaps unintentionally—putting across to its users.

These relationships can pop up in a couple of ways:

- **Sequence:** Which idea comes first, and what comes later
- **Theme**: How ideas are understood when looked at as a group

Sometimes these elements show up in design in ways that are very literal and obvious. In game design, the sequence of a story is the literal structure of the product (though not all games have or require a conventional linear narrative). And the themes are right there in how the game is marketed and sold. In product design, you might have to dig a bit deeper, or look at your product through a marketing lens, to detect its thematic elements. But you'll also see narrative pop up in very straightforward design tools, like user journeys.

Elements of story are hidden in other tools for deconstructing product design too, like system blueprints that tell the entire story of a system in one image. For example, some of my colleagues at Shopify created a blueprint showing all the parts of a developer's experience on Shopify's platform. Like a user journey map, this blueprint illustrates the things a developer experiences, but goes beyond just showing the physical pages they land on along the way. Instead, the blueprint lists all of the services that support the journey. The result is a document that tells the whole story of a developer-focused product, surfacing all of its parts and showing how they relate to one another (**FIG 4.1**).

When we talk about narrative and story in any context, we tend to focus on the text we use to tell that story: the text that's visible in a product interface, for example, or the specific beats of a narrative you might encounter in a game.

But story is, at its heart, architecture. Every narrative form, from movies to short stories to poems, is defined by its structure.

If you look at the structure of any product or system, you can understand the system through narrative—the organization and relationship of concepts, the paths and flows through them, and the way visual patterns support those connections. Looking at a system this way can help us see how a new or changing idea affects that system, just as a new chapter or character might change a traditional story.

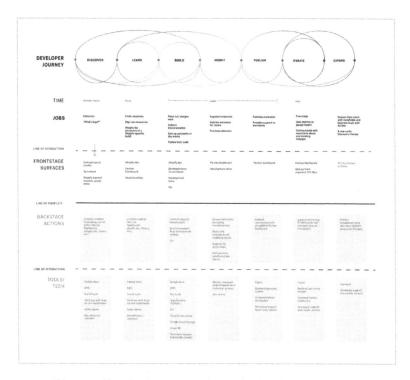

FIG 4.1: This system blueprint document combines a developer's user journey and the tools and services that support it. Image courtesy of Shopify (authors: Hayley Hughes and Andrew Rajaram).

With a digital product, ideas change as they're placed in different contexts across a system. By understanding those contexts through different narrative lenses or ways of seeing the product as a story, we can give more color and shape to that narrative at different points.

We typically think of stories as linear. One thing happens, and then another. But in a digital world, it's possible for stories to be nonlinear. This means a user can encounter the ideas in a story in almost any order. The way they choose to move through a product experience is the way they experience its narrative.

Sometimes a digital experience can lock the user into a linear flow they can't easily leave—as can happen when filling in a form, or going through a sign-up flow. But these are typically brief bursts of bounded experience that get the user to their goal quickly. Once the goal is complete, they can continue making their path through the experience: clicking on links in pages, moving through navigation, and searching for what they need.

System narrative, then, is narrative that is mostly multilinear. But that doesn't mean the author or designer of a product's story doesn't have control over how that story is understood. A product narrative is "written" by a designer who chooses to structure information in a specific way, even though that information is not received in a single, repeatable sequence.

There are lots of ways to see information in a product through a narrative lens. You can see elements of story in:

- The product's information architecture
- The repetition of words or themes across a product
- The user's journey
- The stories visual patterns tell

Understanding and designing with each of these four elements in mind means that a new concept will be supported by and grounded in the system narrative, making it more discoverable, memorable, and effective.

After all of this, a final element transforms the story. Just as a book needs a reader or a play needs an audience, a product experience is ultimately filtered through the user's perspective, by how they understand and engage with it. This is a big topic on its own, and we'll get to it in Chapter 5. For now, keep in mind that narrative is always dependent on its audience.

STORIES IN INFORMATION ARCHITECTURE

Information architecture (IA) tells the story of a product. When you visit a website and look at the top or left-hand navigation, you see an instant snapshot of the story of the product—the features and concepts found there, how they're organized, how different or similar items are grouped together, and how those groups are arranged. The way we group concepts, and what we call those groups, shows up in the filtering options we offer and the primary navigation we present. It also shows up in what we prioritize and what we don't. All of these say: "This is what this product is about, and this is what matters most within it."

The relationships among elements of an IA tell a story, because when similar things are grouped together, implicit narratives will start to form in users' minds about *why* they are related and what those relationships say about the entire product. The act of grouping is a subtle but profound act of making narrative. These relationships can exist across an entire IA, affecting the navigation of a complete product.

Relationships can also exist between specific concepts in the IA. Shopify once had two types of apps: public and private. These two concepts were conceptually similar—they were both types of apps—but in almost every meaningful way, they were different. They looked different, they were built differently, and they were owned by different people.

These two elements were placed together in Shopify's navigation under a top-level navigation item called *Apps*. The placement of these two things together, and the prominence given to that group in the product navigation, told two kinds of stories. It said, "These things are a pair." And it said something about how important apps were to the story of Shopify as a product, and to how it wanted users to see it. (Shopify has moved away from this approach and now allows users to pin specific apps to their left navigation. Still important, but highlighted in a different way.)

The process of creating those groups to tell that story— the work of IA—is a matter of understanding IA concepts in terms of:

- Their differences
- Their similarities
- Their priority or hierarchy in a system
- Their memorability

Finding differences in IA

Every piece of a system is distinct from the pieces around it. While relationships will always exist among those pieces, the differences are what convey that a concept is distinct and crisply defined. If one piece seems too closely related to its siblings, there's a danger of confusion. If it's too much of a one-off, with no clear relationship to any part of a system, it may not be a part of the system at all; it fails the fitness test.

Let's take the messaging product Slack as an example. Slack is a tool used for communication within businesses and organizations. I would say that Slack wants their product to tell a narrative that's more personal than formal—the antidote to more established tools like Microsoft and their rival Teams product. Slack's design choices reinforce this personal narrative by putting the user at the heart of their product story.

First, a user moves through different spaces in Slack, different places for different types of activities (**FIG 4.2**):

- **Workspaces:** This is a governing organizational concept for Slack, because a workspace is the "space" that holds all other Slack tools. When you sign in to Slack, you sign in to a workspace. Your workspaces are organized in a bar on the far left.
- **Apps, direct messages (DMs), and channels.** While they have their differences, these tools make up the typical actions a user takes every day. They inhabit the same spatial zone in the design, collected within a single workspace. You won't find the same DMs, channels, or even apps across other workspaces.

Fundamentally, apps, DMs, and channels are all message threads. Even the apps section takes the form of a message thread between the user and the app. So these different tools share a strong narrative link because they use the same visual and interaction pattern—a classic group-message pattern with a text box at the bottom.

Slack has done a good job of convincing its users of the value of separating these concepts of DMs, threads, and so on. Each menu item within a workspace has some nuanced but crucially

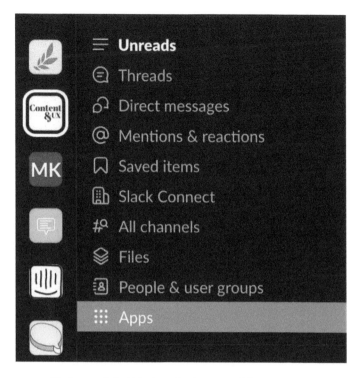

FIG 4.2: Workspaces (left sidebar) are clearly separated from apps, messages, and channels in Slack's interface.

different rules (direct messages with multiple members are always private and by invitation only; channels can be made public, so they can be found by anyone).

Every product has some intentional variation among its features. And these differences tell users a story about how they should think about and use the product. For Slack, there is a fundamental story of *flexibility*—that there are many ways to communicate, and the user can manage their conversations and the functionality around them as they see fit.

There is also a theme of *groups*—that Slack is designed for large groups and for jumping between many conversations in those groups. Including apps is a way of signifying how powerful the platform can become. A messaging platform that only had one type of conversation—that only allowed for DMs, for example—would be telling a very different story about itself.

To understand the elements that tell a story within your own product, you can start by auditing its tools (refer to the content audit discussion in Chapter 1) and analyzing what makes them different. Once you've got your audit ready, you can start to look for commonalities across your concepts, as well as aspects that make them distinct. What you'll be looking for, from a story perspective, is a sense of what those differences and similarities say about your product. They'll show you what matters most to your product and thus what ideas should be foregrounded when you present your product to users.

Seeing similarities in IA

Your product content audit—or perhaps your high-level visual diagram of your product features, if you decide to go in more of a diagram than a spreadsheet direction—is a tool you can return to again and again. Next, you can begin to organize your concepts into groups, finding affinities among certain topics. You'll want to look at exactly how similar things are and whether there are parent/child relationships to consider, which can then be organized into groups and subgroups.

In Slack, the system narrative has a strong element of *user personalization*, which means that a lot of the similarities among things in the same group—between channels, or between direct messages—are established by the user (FIG 4.3). Slack itself provides a visual framework for users to create those clusters.

As you look for affinities, you might also find concepts that are far apart—a channel and an app, for instance—that none-theless have a strong connection.

These distanced connections can be:

- **Functional:** The channel relies on the app to be installed to perform some basic functionality to keep the channel running smoothly.

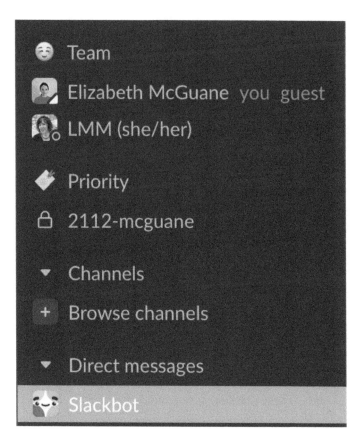

FIG 4.3: Slack allows users to create personalized sections like the "Team" and "Priority" sections shown here, identified by a user-selected emoji. They sit at the same level of hierarchy as the "Channels" and "Direct messages" sections generated by the app.

- **Semantic:** Two concepts might sound similar but do very different things. (In a user-editable IA like Slack's, this is par for the course, with many channels sharing similar names.)

Analyzing the similarities between concepts establishes both necessary affinities and unintended connections across the system—connections that might confuse users.

Assessing these connections also shines a light on new dimensions of a system. By pattern-matching topics that exist across multiple surfaces, the system can be seen in new ways.

Auditing and diagramming your concepts are not the only ways to continue this investigation into the story your IA is telling. Different styles of user research will give you even more perspective on your narrative because they'll give you other humans' perspectives on a system that by now is probably very familiar to you. Card sorting exercises, which ask users to group topics presented on either digital or physical cards, are a classic research method that can help you see how users would organize concepts according to their similarities and differences.

When conducting a card sorting exercise (or any other IA-focused user test), aim to record a user's feedback as they complete the test. Often it is their comments on the experience, and not just the results of their grouping, that provide the most valuable context for the design team. The comments will show whether users understand the concepts they're grouping, and will illuminate why they've chosen to organize them in certain ways.

Considering IA hierarchy

Establishing hierarchy—deciding which elements are more important than others in a given design, or indeed in any system—is the most important part of any IA exercise. It can also be the most difficult because it can be highly subjective. It requires judgment calls about the order of relationships across your concepts, as well as their relative importance. But you'll also need to make a call about how much your system should enforce that hierarchy, over and above a user's own preferences.

If we think back to the idea that Slack wants to present its product narrative as one that is personal and even personable, it becomes apparent that the app's designers have made some subtle decisions about the hierarchy of objects within a Slack workspace. Users can control relationships by reorganizing aspects of their workspace, dragging and dropping their channels and direct messages into different positions in the navigation menu, and moving items between sections.

FIG 4.4: The items at the top of Slack's navigation ("Unreads," "Direct messages," "Mentions & reactions," etc.) are not as easily reordered by the user as the channels and apps below this section. Slack made an intentional narrative choice here.

Only a few elements at the very top of the left navigation can't be easily moved through drag and drop (**FIG 4.4**). But that difference, that choice to change the ease of access, conveys something very important about the system narrative Slack has created. It says that Slack is more opinionated about what things appear at the very top of their navigation, and in what order, and—even if they do allow the user to change that order in their account settings—they are telling a story through the default order they choose to display to new users. Although they're exerting more control, they're doing so to keep the app focused on individual users and their behavior. You can see this in the choice of elements they include at the top of their nav:

- An individual's unread messages, one-to-one direct messages, and mentions and reactions to messages sent by that user come first.
- Items that focus on group communication, like channels— though they are likely a highly visited type of thread in Slack—appear lower in the menu.

This sequence tells a story about how Slack wants users to see it—a story that's not a simple matter of looking to data to see which sections are visited most. It's a story that says that what sits at the center of Slack is not the group or teams you're part of, but you: the user. (Funnily enough, "Mentions & reactions" might not be visited much at all, as Slack's notification functionality is designed to bring the user directly to a specific mention of their name right in the thread where it happened.)

To analyze your own product hierarchy, return to your audit or diagram. You might find that some of your similar groups naturally sit alongside one another, like siblings. When looking at the hierarchy of concepts within each group, consider: Which names and topics matter most to your entire audience? Which are valuable to a more niche set of users? Which concepts go together in pairs, or trios? Which ones need to be understood first in a flow, so that other concepts can be grasped?

When thinking about hierarchy and priority, the key element to consider is: Priority *for whom*? Priorities might change depending on which customer is using the product, so having a sense of who the target users are is an absolute must before any of this work happens.

Even more crucial will be whether you're making a narrative decision because of business or brand priorities. Hierarchy is often a subjective judgment call about the message a business wants to send. As Slack did, a company will sometimes decide to raise a certain concept to the highest level because of the story it tells about the product as a whole. Research and data studies that tell you who users are, and which pages they're already visiting, must be considered when thinking about hierarchy— but they won't provide the whole story.

Is your IA memorable?

Finally, a good IA is a memorable one: one that tells a story whose parts—its beginning, middle, and end, its key characters and relationships—can be recalled without a visual reminder. Slack is a good example of a powerful, complex IA. This is most evident through the power of its search menu, or, more accurately, its "Jump to" navigation menu.

Quietly prominent at the very top of every Slack window, the "Jump to" menu allows users to navigate by keywords and memory across all the channels, messages, and apps in their workspace—which can number in the thousands (**FIG 4.5**).

Power users of Slack, those who use it daily, have internalized Slack's narrative such that they can rely on search to quickly move through its layers of hierarchy and across similar and different concepts within the IA, without needing to use the left navigation at all.

Not every product is as complex, or complex in the same way, as Slack and other rich messaging applications. Not all of them ask us to hold a customized IA in our minds at all times. (Indeed, it's a marvel of interaction that Slack works as well as it does, given how malleable its IA is in support of its product story of being customizable.) But any product can aim to have its users internalize its key concepts by understanding the elements of the story the product is telling. When a narrative is this strong, users can recreate and navigate to them without relying on a visual navigation menu.

A good test for this sense of memorability takes us back to the mental-model drawing exercises discussed in Chapter 1. By sketching out the concepts that naturally spring to mind when users (or your own colleagues) think about your product, you'll get a sense of how memorable your information architecture is, and how much of your product narrative can be held in a person's mind when they're not looking at its interface. We can't expect users to recall every concept in a product. And because product narratives are nonlinear, people will likely remember concepts and tools in your product from very different vantage points—and even from different starting and end points—for their drawing, telling different stories about

FIG 4.5: In Slack's "Jump to" menu, users can locate specific items without using the left navigation. For example, searching for a user by name quickly brings up their profile.

them. But even understanding that variance in mental models is hugely valuable, because the story in the user's mind is ultimately what wins.

STORIES FOUND IN PIECES

Thinking about search in Slack is a great way to start thinking about the pieces of a system narrative that are divorced from their context and separated across a product experience. This is how ideas are experienced by a user as they move through a product experience. Concepts will show up not in a single menu, but on pages and screens separated across space and experienced across time, depending on how frequently and deeply the product is used by that person. Think of this way of encountering ideas in pieces as a narrative lens of modularity, or seeing the parts of a story as reusable blocks.

Modularity means that the elements you build with—whether code or bricks, sentences or visual patterns—are self-contained enough that they can be used anywhere and can stand alone if necessary. Thinking in modules—in terms of repeated, reusable parts—is common in fields like engineering and architecture. In product design, it's common to any discussion of design systems and the components and patterns they contain.

But words themselves can be modular, too. Especially in interface design, it's useful to think about the words on the screen as recyclable "chunks" that you can use again and again.

Not every word you write in an interface will work this way, of course. Some content you create will be unique because there's no need to repeat it. And there'll be places where you'll want to vary how you say something just to keep the interface from sounding too robotic. But interface content can generally withstand more repetition than most forms of writing (aside from, say, road signs or subway maps).

When this modularity happens at the sentence level, and terms and phrases are repeated across a product, it makes the product feel coherent and clear, building on the narrative laid out by your information architecture—just like chapters at the beginning of a book set the stage for the story that follows.

The reason modularity is such a useful approach—whether it happens in your code base, in your design system and visual patterns, or in your words themselves—is that it turns a product into a system of reusable parts rather than a sequence of standalone screens. When you make your content modular, you can extend the boundaries of that system beyond your product, using the same terms and phrases in your help content, your marketing, and anywhere you're trying to express your product story. All of this means that your product's story will become easier for your team to tell, since you won't be reinventing the wheel every time you try to express an idea in a new location. And that means your story will feel more unified and whole wherever your users encounter it.

Modularity across different interfaces

Understanding conceptual relationships is fundamental for designers, but it's also fundamental for technical product builders like engineers and data scientists. When engineers design an API—which is essentially a means of communicating programmatically with an application without needing to go through an interface (it's an interface without a face, so to speak)—deciding which things to group together is very much an information architecture task.

What makes an API different—and sometimes masks its role as a form of IA—is that it's designed to be used in discrete pieces. Developers building on an API can glean a product story from your API documentation if they read it in full. (And by the way, API documentation is a great resource for anyone modeling product hierarchies and relationships.) But developers are far more likely to access only the API element they need for the functionality they're building.

API design also requires being able to think of each piece of a product discretely—letting products be coherently designed within themselves, rather than creating experiences that seem glued together from a kit of parts.

Modularity requires understanding concepts as they're organized in the data layer of a product, in APIs. It can be found in the data created by and about those concepts, the metrics and insights about them. And it can be found in the data that a platform generates—the data that machine-learning products learn from.

Data is really the fuel of modular narratives, because it connects elements across different spaces and dimensions, and allows different ways of seeing a product narrative—metanarratives about the product—to become part of its story.

All of this can rapidly become very abstract and hard to tie down to something that can easily influence how a design team might think about a concept. It can help to start with the most basic of basics—to return to words. Breaking down a system in terms of the *words that express it* makes it possible to clarify just what each concept is: a collection of words. From there, a narrative path can be built on top of clear, modular elements.

Modularity in language

We've seen how an idea or concept can repeat itself, and the way it's phrased or structured can be repeated as well. This creates modular chunks of language that create their own themes and narrative links across a system. If you look closely at any product, you'll see that themes are conveyed at the sentence level, just as they are at the topic or IA level.

For example, think of an app store platform—Apple or Google, say. The app store provides users with various applications, or apps, presented visually as icons. Each app contains sets of information specific to that app. The language referencing the app will change depending on where you are in a flow. For example, when you first see a set of suggested apps, the information presented is minimal (FIG 4.6). After you click on the

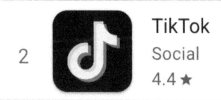

FIG 4.6: When first navigating through an app store, the app appears in a list of many others and comes with only a small amount of content (icon, name, rating).

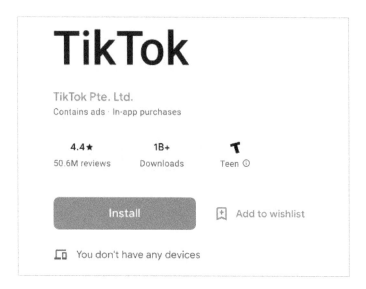

FIG 4.7: After selecting an app from a list in the app store, additional content is revealed (company information, downloads, etc.), as well as common words and phrases such as the "Install" call to action.

app listing, you are provided with some of the same information, alongside more context about the app to help you understand what you're downloading (**FIG 4.7**). You can think of this as expanding a module of information to provide more content. The fact that some language remains consistent helps you identify that you're still looking at the same concept, just a richer version of it.

Each time the app appears, the name of the app and its logo are repeated, but we also see certain word modules or content patterns begin to repeat:

Metadata like the app's average star rating, how many downloads it has, or its age rating

- Calls to action like "Install"
- Supporting information such as whether the user has any devices connected to their account

These content patterns tell a story about what you can do on this app store, not just with this app but with any similar app you visit. The patterns start to build up a narrative about how this app store functions, allowing you to install and use software it contains. They also reveal information about what the app store values by including general context about quality (star ratings), and also personal context about the user ("you don't have any devices" text).

Each of these content modules can be added to any app listing page, and users will begin to expect and look for that information even if they've never visited a specific app's listing page before.

How to find the pieces of your product story

Making concepts modular is a feat of imagination. It's a process of visualizing a concept beyond a single interface or flow and imagining all the other places that concept might appear, and what patterns will house it.

Taking a set of ideas and turning them into a set of modular text elements is, if you have a detail-oriented bent, kind of fun. Here are some practical ways you can get started:

- **Examine the nouns (objects) and verbs (tools or actions)** visible in your interface, and catalog them in an audit. This will become a macro view of the modular text elements across your whole product and within specific topic areas, flows, or even single pages (FIG 4.8). You can find these objects and actions in the interface itself and by looking at the navigation menu. A list of features will give you the names (or nouns) within your system, and calls to action and links on each page will provide you with your set of common verbs (or actions).

- **Look at the descriptive content** you use to support your product beyond just names and actions—basically, anything not contained in a page title or a call-to-action button. Take some notes about the content you're using to convey an idea in your interface. Are you varying how you describe the same idea in different places? Are there opportunities to make your content more reusable and consistent?
- **Test different ways of expressing an idea** in your interface. Vary your calls to action, as well as the phrases you use to describe a feature, to see how users respond when certain phrases come to the fore. This will help you create a linguistic system for a concept that you know users will respond well to.

What you're doing here is deconstructing the story your product is telling, by looking for nouns, verbs, and descriptive phrases. By pulling these elements of text out of your interface, you can start to see where you're varying the way you tell your story. Then, you can determine whether that variation is justified or not.

If you're struggling to get started with mapping out this text-based version of your product, start by looking for nouns in the menus and page titles in your interface, as well as the objects listed in your product's APIs. Look for actions in your links and button text, where you'll see verbs repeated. For descriptive text, look at introductions in your pages, or look to see how you describe features in your help content or even how you verbally tell the story of your product in conversations with customers.

It's wonderful how much can be understood about a product just by isolating parts of speech. You can quickly establish the nouns that describe your users, as well as the nouns that describe your product's features and objects. These nouns form

FIG 4.8: A framework for a product audit can help with categorizing the elements that appear in a system, making it more than a list of feature names.

the baseline narrative of your product—your cast of characters, so to speak.

This cast of characters will appear in many places across your product. The ones that are mentioned most are the star players in the story you're telling. Simply by seeing them this way, divorced from their interfaces or other contexts, you can get a strong sense of the story at play. This gives you a better sense of how to deploy these characters in any future journey you design within your product.

STORIES IN A USER'S JOURNEY

Once you understand your ideas and content as modular blocks—nouns as objects, verbs as actions—it becomes easier to create a narrative path through a product, even before the experience has been designed as an interface.

But the user's context is what matters most when you're thinking about how to knit these modular pieces back together. The amount of context the user has when visiting a specific screen in your product will affect how much information they need you to provide. And the context you have about the user—

what device they're using, what sort of journey they're on, and what their expectations are of the experience—will help you consider how to lay out that information along their journey in the best way for them to receive it.

A specific user's journey or path—the "plot" of your product as users experience it—will show up in your product in a few ways. First, a path will show up as the set of *modular objects* and concepts users experience through your content, navigation, page titles, and calls to action. It will also show up in the form of repeated visual patterns you use to tell the story, which we'll get to shortly, but you don't need to start by choosing visual patterns to figure out what your story should be.

In fact, sketching out potential user journeys or paths before designing an interface provides a clear guide for the later up-close, visual design work to follow. Paths provide key information, such as:

- How many steps a journey requires
- What the hierarchy of those steps is
- Where objects encounter other objects in a system
- How the user should feel at each point in the journey

Starting by plotting a path acknowledges the three-dimensional nature of products, rather than the two-dimensional nature of interfaces. Designers have to think about the steps a user will take through the product, and parcel out the information they'll need at each step, as well as the time it will take them to complete an action—rather than the visual experience they'll encounter while doing so.

A user journey must take a specific type of user through a series of connected points, in a specific order, to a specific end. These are the plot points in a story, and every path constructed this way needs to feel coherent in its own context, both as the user is experiencing it and as part of a wider whole. An object-driven path through an interface can represent objects in a few different ways, but there are two that represent different extremes:

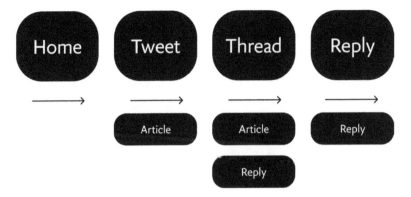

FIG 4.9: Twitter objects such as articles and replies recur throughout the system narrative.

- Plotting nouns that represent object types
- Plotting the story the user moves through

Let's use Twitter as an example. Moving from Twitter's Home screen, through a tweet thread, and into a reply to the original tweet is a relatively simple path. Certain objects, such as articles and replies, occur more than once in that path (**FIG 4.9**).

This narrative begins to show how the experience of Twitter, for the user, is both linear (the user can easily move from Home to a tweet and its responses) and recursive. Elements of the story play out again and again. The experience of using Twitter, with conversations nested inside conversations, bears this out.

Another way to plot the narrative of objects is by *telling the story aloud*. I believe many of us do this organically when describing a visual user journey—that is, we describe the stages of the journey aloud—but it can be particularly eye-opening to challenge yourself to do so without any visual aids.

When you're investigating experiences and figuring out how to make them better, narrative is a great way to analyze their efficiency. A content design colleague of mine does an exercise where she and the designer she's working with simply describe the flow to each other—as if they were giving directions to someone who was lost.

This is how that might go if we were describing the Twitter interface:

1. On the first screen, you can see all the tweets that have been sent lately, and one particular tweet might catch your eye. Maybe it's by someone you admire, or maybe it's something you find funny, or alarming, or interesting.
2. You click on that tweet—called an *article* in Twitter's object model—and now you can see that tweet with all the tweets that are replying directly to it. You can see who has replied in chronological order.
3. You can also see where you can reply. There's a reply below the tweet by someone you know. So you click on it.
4. Now you can see that reply with its own replies beneath it.
5. Those replies might have their own replies, and so on. At every point, you can jump into the conversation with your own reply.

The choose-your-own-adventureness of products is laid bare when you describe them this way. You'll start to see them less as a set of screens, and more as a set of branches and potential ends to a story. Thinking of a user experience in this way is much truer to life than seeing it in terms of its happy path—the idealized trajectory you might want a user to take. This is a very detailed way of looking at narrative—one that's more like breaking out the beats of a story as a screenwriter might—by thinking of the user as a character at the center of it all, with choices to make.

By speaking the narrative aloud, we can also simplify our language. When we tell a story, what tends to come to the fore are not the places where things happen (the objects we can see on a screen), but rather the actions users take—the way they move through a product over time. By speaking a narrative we can also see how repetitive those actions are, and therefore how unified our choices about interaction design should be. Compared with visual exploration, which is static until we build a working prototype, the spoken word is a wonderfully accessible way to access the movement that is part of every interactive experience.

No matter how you approach your exploration of narrative, you'll find that every product path you design can be broken down into a set of nouns and verbs and then described narratively. A product that you can't tell a simple story about will also be difficult for your users to find their way around. Like characters wandering into a dark forest in a fairy tale, users may end up hopelessly lost.

STORIES IN VISUAL PATTERNS

Understanding the objects in your system gives you a nonvisual way of describing a path through a concept, step by step. The experience of a narrative will always be at least somewhat absorbed as a visual experience, supported by visual design patterns.

Describing a path can also directly influence later visual choices, making it easier to select certain patterns at each stage of a path so that the user is led not just through an information narrative that makes sense, but also through a visual narrative that feels coherent within a given product. Every path should ideally make use of consistent actions and patterns: a tweet should always look like a tweet, a reply like a reply. The difference between objects that are similar, yet have distinct differences, must also manifest in their visual presentation.

A typical visual pattern through a product will move among patterns, and those patterns will be repeated over and over. Visual patterns support a narrative progression by being consistent. And visual consistency is something that can be understood implicitly. From childhood onward, humans know to put square wooden blocks in square holes, and triangles within triangles.

This might seem relatively simple, but matching a well-defined concept to a consistent visual pattern can be tricky. At Shopify, there was a redesign of the Settings section of the product. This area housed a lot of content, and the team decided it should live in a layer of its own. This required creating a new pattern, one that would contain every settings page, with its own menu to navigate through.

FIG 4.10: There is a huge amount of content in this settings area, and it needs a visual pattern that will help users navigate that content easily.

Settings are not normally a highly visually prominent space in a product. They're utilitarian by nature. The tricky thing was that Shopify's settings housed a lot of important tasks that its users needed to access infrequently—but when they did, the workflows they needed to move through went several levels deep (**FIG 4.10**).

So, the aim was to design a space that users could:

- Access from anywhere
- Understand and configure quickly
- Leave and return easily to their previous location

The previous design housed content under a complex menu embedded in a page, which required users to travel back and forth between that menu and the pages beneath it to discover the content they needed. Having a left navigation—something that would let them see both categories and content at the same time—seemed like a great way to solve that problem. A

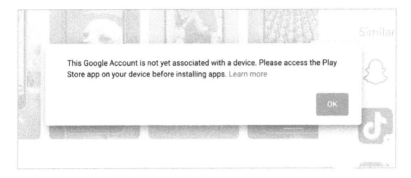

FIG 4.11: Small overlay modals, like this Google example, are often used for dead ends or actions that take the user off their primary narrative path.

left navigation also meant the visual design pattern needed to be full-screen: an overlay.

Shopify already had a number of overlay patterns at that time. Overlays are a common pattern in digital products because they let the user move into action without losing their place in the product's narrative. Overlays can be small, like modals that ask you to confirm a single action or acknowledge a dead end (**FIG 4.11**). Overlays can also be large, like editing experiences that ask you to choose colors, images, and type for your new website (**FIG 4.12**). Shopify had both of those.

Editing a theme is a deeply focused and creative action. The visual pattern it uses has its own left-hand navigation, and its screen takes over the primary Shopify interface. It lifts the user up and away from the Shopify product itself. This is by design: users spend a lot of time editing a theme in one sitting.

Finding and configuring a setting is quite a different task. Settings patterns most often focus on speed—it should fundamentally take less time to configure something once than to edit a website. In Shopify's case, though some settings were complex and technical, most could be completed in minutes. The primary work of the day was still done elsewhere in the Shopify app.

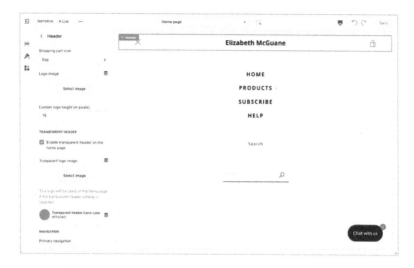

FIG 4.12: A large overlay, like Shopify's full-screen theme editor, allows users to spend focused time adjusting visual details without interruption.

So instead of a full screen, the team designed something subtly different: a drawer that users could pull up from the bottom of the screen. The drawer could be accessed from anywhere: from search results, from Shopify's primary navigation, or from text within a page (**FIG 4.11**). It was this understanding of where a user might access settings across many narrative paths that influenced the team's pattern selection.

Patterns tell a story that is not limited to their visual appearance. If you compare the appearance of the theme editor and the settings pattern, the two have a lot in common. Both are large and take over all or part of the screen. Both cover the product's primary navigation. But the story they tell is about their utility—how they behave—and the content each one supports. Users need different navigation mechanisms to move into and across editing and configuration experiences. That means the design patterns that support those experiences do fundamentally different things, and therefore need subtle variations. They're two similar spaces that house different ideas and ways of working.

Visual patterns tell a story about how a product works to its users. By using an identical pattern in a completely different part of an application, you create a conceptual link between two different things. Using the same pattern tells the user: "These things are alike, and you can expect certain things to happen here." So it's vital to think about visual patterns and relationships from a conceptual point of view, and not just in terms of their form factor or visual details.

THE ESSENCE OF STORY

Narrative is the way humans see the world, in small ways and big ways. It's how most of us figure things out and store memories. All of the topics this book has covered so far—understanding an idea, creating new metaphors, coming up with names—can be understood and evaluated through the lens of story.

Further decisions can be made about a product's story by analyzing its navigation paths, information groupings, and visual patterns, as tools for representing narrative.

Defining a concept without placing it in a narrative is like having a wonderful idea for a story without knowing what form it will take. By analyzing narrative, a design team can start making decisions that will lock that story into a specific format. Like making a choice between a short story and a novel, or an article and a screenplay, it's a matter of accepting a framework that a product will need to follow. Each designer going through this process must create their own narrative rules. Those rules will support—or complicate—every future design decision they make.

5 HOW TO BE UNDERSTOOD

MANY DESIGNERS APPROACH A DESIGN problem by exploring visual patterns and seeing what narrative directions are inspired by the visual elements that seem appropriate, or that are readily available in a UI kit or design system. It's natural to move toward what can be seen and explored spatially, and there's nothing wrong with this approach, as long as it doesn't lead the design down paths that are difficult to return from. There are many starting points and on- and off-ramps in the design process, and visual patterns can become a locked-in view of the possible solutions available for a given concept.

A visual solution should foreground what needs to be communicated about a concept above all else. Understanding the layers of meaning and metaphor beneath the product, via a process distinct from the visual design patterns that might express it, encourages a thoughtful and intentional use of those patterns. The result is a finished design that is more fundamentally sound. Though this might feel like a delay on the way to the so-called "real" work of design, it is often design's best first step. Finding a certain dexterity in communication before being locked into specific patterns can speed up iterations of design and prevent creative blocks.

These various facets of communication, language, and visual design are what bring your defined concept to life. When you're executing and building, your focus won't be on abstract concepts and metaphors but on the reality of what your users will see on a screen. This is the bridge from idea to reality, the nuts and bolts of putting a design together in real terms—how it is explained, up close, in specific screens. It's a matter of asking: Is this concept clearly communicated? How is it structured and expressed on the screen? What does it express? How much does it say, and is it likely to be understood?

Putting the design together also often requires working within the bounds of a design system. In Chapter 4, we saw how important it is to make sure a pattern faithfully supports a concept and its narrative goals. That means, too, that design teams need to be empowered to explore a broad spectrum of visual expression so they can form arguments for breaking with the past and making something new.

SETTING COMMUNICATION GOALS

All design exists to communicate an idea. Because I'm a writer, I tend to start by seeing communication through text. Not all communication happens through text, of course, but it's a useful way to evaluate how well an idea is coming across because it reduces the task of design into a simple, powerful element: words.

A design can be understood as a narrative; we've already talked about how to use tools like diagrams to sketch out those narratives at a high level. To really get into the nuts and bolts of what you're trying to communicate, you can use words to describe that narrative in detail, breaking down your story for each page or screen. Think of it as outlining your design like you would an essay or any other structured piece of writing; by removing visual distractions, you can establish that you've got the right ideas in the right order.

To assess what information, in what sequence, will provide the foundation for a successful design, you should consider:

- What the user needs to know in each moment
- How to structure and arrange that information
- What the user will expect of the communication and how they will respond to it

Communication that hits the sweet spot between what a user *needs to know*, what they *expect to find*, and what they *will actually grasp* is the hallmark of a successful interface—or really, of any form of communication.

What does the user need to know?

In our discussion of narrative, we talked about how to structure a path by understanding the pieces of narrative you have available: concepts, relationships and groupings. In applying those tools to a solution, you'll need to consider *how much* of each piece of narrative needs to be presented to the user along the way. Think of that narrative as an outline—the next stage is to write the story.

Still, how much "story" can users absorb at one time? If we put ourselves in the user's shoes, we can see that they experience the story of a product as they move through it. They absorb it in small ways through visual and linguistic cues; at each moment, they use that understanding to make choices about which direction they need to take next—a choose-your-own-adventure story we all embark on whenever we use software.

With so many paths a user can take, it's vital that ideas be broken down and presented to them in small portions. More experienced users may be able to understand the deeper architecture of a product's narrative—if they're building something, for example.

It's important to remember that beyond the specific screen or feature being designed, the user will already have formed an impression of your product from marketing and information architecture. It's as though you're writing a screenplay—you can assume the user will have already watched the trailer about the movie and so will have high-level information in mind as you write each scene.

If you're confident the user has already encountered your key concepts through IA and marketing, you can be more selective about how much to communicate in the precise moment or sequence you're designing.

To articulate the information you need to focus on, you can always ask these two questions:

- What happened before this screen?
- What's going to happen next?

Marking out the moment you're trying to communicate makes for a clearer design because it keeps the focus on what matters *now*. It keeps you from needless repetition and redundancy. Once you have the information you need to design your scene or sequence, you can go one level deeper and start the actual work of writing the content for a given screen.

Structuring content in the interface

There is great power in an interface where every word pulls its weight. A good content designer writes well; a great one writes as little as possible. Just as you might be careful not to overload a design with too many icons or visual elements, you can develop an eye for the right balance of text. Think of text as a luxury; indeed, in a mobile context, this is not a choice but a necessity.

A designer must trust that the words they use are necessary to the communication of an idea, that the idea cannot be communicated through other means than text, and that the text doesn't duplicate or explain what the UI already communicates. Text is a visual element and a part of the design language—just as space, proximity, hierarchy, and so forth are a part of it. While an interface would likely not be intelligible without words, the words are just one chord being played, not the entire song.

Explaining the interface is a common stumbling block because it can feel helpful and correct to do so. Whenever you introduce a new concept to a system, it can be tempting to add text to explain it—perhaps with information icons, tooltips, or banners. In some cases, these supporting text elements simply

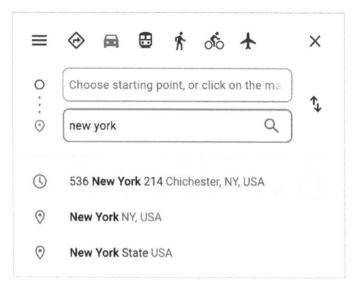

FIG 5.1: A modeled input field understands how to translate simple text into a specific format: an address.

duplicate what the design is already doing: letting the user discover the feature utility through interaction.

It's all about balance. Some text support might be necessary, but challenge yourself to see if you can deliver a new concept implicitly, rather than supplementing all of the UI with education. Not all in-product explanation and education is wrong, but some education comes from trusting the design to do the explaining on its own. The user will gather knowledge by experience, rather than by being told how it should work. This is the way most of us learn and understand new products and features, from knowing we need to press a lever to lower bread into a toaster, to knowing we need to click—or tab—through fields to fill in an online form.

For example, imagine an input field that interprets specific types of data in a specific format. This could be a date field with a certain day-month-year order, a phone number field that needs to separate area code from number, or a map field that can translate a few keywords into a destination (**FIG 5.1**).

Challenge yourself to let the field do the work of explaining how to format it rather than using help text. If this is done right, the interface can start to feel to the user like it is responding to their internal monologue. They begin to use the tool on their own, rather than feeling like someone is looking over their shoulder, teaching them how to use something.

This aim of reducing text and relying on intuition applies to names and concepts as well. Sometimes the UI doesn't need to be littered with them. Not everything needs to be labeled.

Placing words in space

Words are a form of visual and verbal communication, and therefore they occupy space—they're material. Understanding text as a material element as well as a semantic one is a big part of understanding it as a form of expression. Expression is all about the fit and finish of the final product—the way all the conceptual work and design detail come together in the words expressed in the interface.

The expression of language is often defined as its "tone of voice." Yet tone doesn't just come from the words themselves and how they sound, how playful or formal their effect is—it's also conveyed by the visual design of an interface, and how matched or mismatched the verbal and visual tone are to each other. Tone is less a matter of copywriting skill than an aggregation of what the user sees and what they hear when they glance at an interface. The design generates a feeling.

Proximity and space

Figuring out which items to group closely together in an interface is the first step toward making sure your design can communicate well and will be understood. When two elements sit in proximity to each other, they tell a story to the user about the relationship between them. They tell the user: *These are of similar importance,* or, *You should use these things in the same way.*

For example, elements placed at the top of a screen tell the user: "This is the thing you'll do most often." Elements hidden behind a menu say: "These will be used less frequently." The

FIG 5.2: Help text positioned below the field is read after the user tries to interact—or is not read at all.

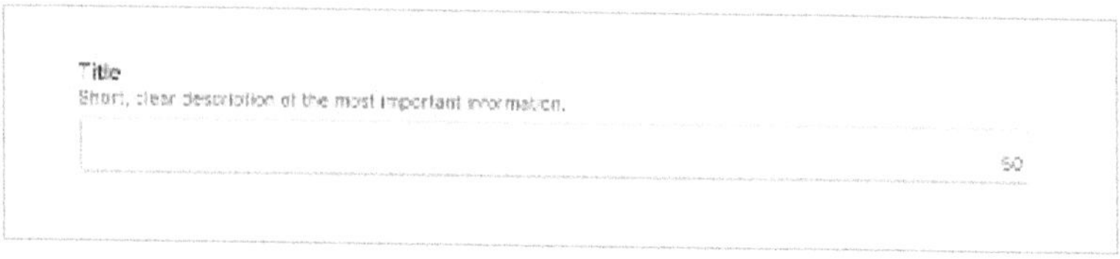

Title
Short, clear description of the most important information.
50

FIG 5.3: Help text positioned above the field provides a subtle advantage in reading order—and increases the odds that a user will actually read it.

position does the job of communicating importance without interface text needing to call it out.

This means that editing information in an interface isn't only about the words you write, but where they sit in a space—their juxtaposition. What lives close to what, what lives above and below what, and how much "what" there is overall—all of these editorial choices contribute to how the user perceives a design and gets meaning from it.

Here's a simple example from my own work: a text field accompanied by a label (describing what the field is) and help text (giving context about how it should be used). A designer on my team changed the standard field pattern, in which the help text appeared below the field, so that the help text appeared between the label and the field (**FIG 5.2-3**). Their argument made a lot of sense. Reading the content felt like it flowed better when looking at the field.

Sighted users are unlikely to read in linear order, so the position of the text plays a role in how it's evaluated. Placing the help text above the field raises the prominence of help text from a subordinate to a dominant role. Even in this simple example, the position of text—how it lives in space—plays a huge part in how users might interpret its meaning and value.

We want our decisions about orientation, juxtaposition, and space to be implicit. We want our information to make sense and our grouping of that information to be intuitive. We want it to be blindingly obvious to the user why we've made something the primary detail—the largest thing on the screen—so that they understand why they should go there. And we want our idea of the most important thing to match the user's goal.

Visual patterns and the use of space are the means you use to represent relationships to users. Choosing similar design patterns for similar problems and concepts; making the most important things big, or colorful, or prominent; and grouping similar concepts close together in navigation or on a page—all of these are visual tools that rest on a clear sense of the relationships and priorities you've encoded in the system.

Language is part of these spaces, of course, but it's also part of the apparatus you use to describe how these patterns work. The concepts of similarity, difference, and priority are defined in words, and they're relative.

Keeping it simple

Many products have technical and complex concepts within them. But watch out for a tendency to overexplain these concepts, especially if your product has different audiences.

To ward off that inclination, try describing the interface aloud, as we did in Chapter 4 during our discussion of object-driven paths. Start by verbally describing a feature and walking through the story of how it would be used. (It helps to do this in pairs, but recording yourself and playing it back will also work if you're designing solo.)

Listening to the way you describe the flow will help you pay attention not only to the language you're using, but also to the sequencing of information and the point where you start to feel the need for diagrams or visual aids. The story you tell should simplify your design. We have a natural tendency to pare down information in spoken language, and any lack of clear sequence or organization should become clear as you speak. You can then incorporate that simplicity into your visual design and user flows.

When we think about content design, we tend to dwell on the word "content." We think of it as a task focused on words alone. But most effective content design work focuses on space and structure, as much or even more than on words.

In general, content in an interface is there to help the user move through an experience. It's not there to make them stop and read. It should give users the help they need when they need it, but never say too much. One content designer I spoke to described their perspective on content as being about consideration and kindness toward the user, which is a great way to think about it. Never add content to an interface to fill a space—always think about how much information is needed to clearly communicate.

Which words are essential?

Great editing means focusing on what really needs to be said, saying it as simply as possible, and then ruthlessly and repeatedly paring that back. There are a few different ways to do this:

- **Focus:** Cut away anything irrelevant to the user's communication goal.
- **Be consistent:** Set and follow content guidelines across your system—especially for the names and actions in labels and buttons—to speed up user comprehension of your interface. Ideally the only *new* information in an interface is the content that's relevant to your topic alone.
- **Use the full design tool kit:** Most text in the interface can be minimized far more than it is, and sometimes can be removed outright. Consider where you can replace text with interactive or visual elements that communicate an idea, action, or topic. Communication is not only about words, but also ideas.

Not all interfaces are equal, of course, and the volume of explanation needed varies from place to place. For example, some interfaces are bounded by time (messaging apps, for

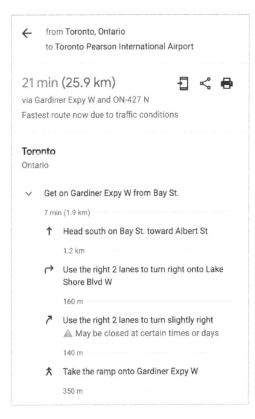

from Toronto, Ontario
to Toronto Pearson International Airport

21 min (25.9 km)

via Gardiner Expy W and ON-427 N
Fastest route now due to traffic conditions

Toronto
Ontario

˅   Get on Gardiner Expy W from Bay St.

7 min (1.9 km)

↑   Head south on Bay St. toward Albert St

1.2 km

↱   Use the right 2 lanes to turn right onto Lake
    Shore Blvd W

160 m

↗   Use the right 2 lanes to turn slightly right
    ⚠ May be closed at certain times or days

140 m

↟   Take the ramp onto Gardiner Expy W

350 m

FIG 5.4: Point-by-point directions, like these from Google Maps, can be overwhelming when read together. They're best experienced step by step as you travel.

instance) and some interfaces are not, and the user controls how quickly they move through it.

Take, for example, point-by-point directions in a GPS. They contain large volumes of information communicated chronologically over time and experienced sequentially (**FIG 5.4**). Because they're written as though you're getting verbal instruction, the volume of text isn't overwhelming.

But an interface that can be traversed in multiple directions at the user's discretion, or even one that happens in a single view (like a simple form), is meant to be communicated at one point in time (**FIG 5.5**). When someone looks at it, they should readily understand it.

HOW TO BE UNDERSTOOD   **101**

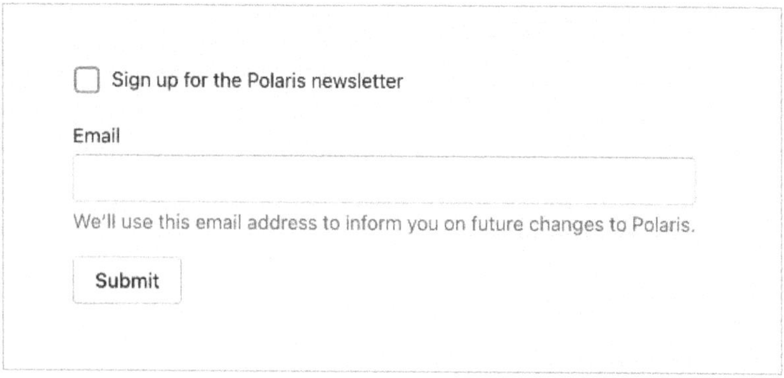

FIG 5.5: A simple, single-field sign-up form needs very little content—its structure makes its intent clear.

When you think about how much needs to be said, it can help to consider real-world comparisons for your interface (recall some of the metaphorical connections we made in Chapter 2). What real-world content is echoed in your interface, and how are those metaphorical siblings connected? Is your interface more like a book that can be read in one sitting, or more like a conversation with several steps? Is it more visual with limited text like a road sign, or more explanatory and long-winded like a recipe?

In nonlinear experiences with many different possible routes, it's safe to disclose information progressively. With product design, there can be a desire to overexplain, even by bringing contextual help into products in the form of popups or tooltips that describe what the interface is trying to say. This is more advisable if you are doing something bounded by time—a form, a survey, or a conversation.

A conversational interface has very deliberate constraints on the volume of text that surrounds it—but text is also completely vital to the experience because the visual design is extremely constrained.

In a support tool, users—customer support agents—are also engaged in a conversation but need a slightly more complex interface (**FIG 5.6**). Their experience, like their end user's, is

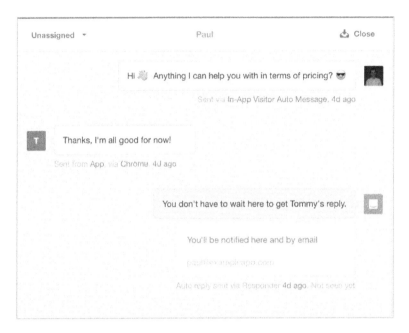

FIG 5.6: The support agent's side of the conversation in Intercom.

asynchronous—the conversation can have replies spaced out over time, and it delivers information to users in pieces.

Giving a support agent extra contextual help within the frame of a conversation, rather than providing "learn more" links to go somewhere else, helps them respond to that conversation more quickly. They need to stay in the narrative as much as possible to make the end user, the person reaching out for help, feel supported and cared for—and to move through their support conversations at a good clip. So it helps to design an interface that feels like it has anticipated what support agents need and can deliver that content to them in one place, rather than sending them somewhere else.

These experiences differ from classic web-app interfaces that a user can move through at their own pace. In those cases, designs should aim for focus and allow the user a more self-directed journey through the screens of the app.

Working on a conversational interface was probably my most creative and joyful period as a designer because it demanded laser precision for every detail, and even every character. So much in a conversational interface is communicated through the passage of time, through motion (and sometimes sound), through the positioning and color of a few very simple visual elements, and through the text itself. It made me fall in love with the way a seemingly simple design pattern can mask great intricacy and nuance.

The volume or style of content in a design, and where it's housed, is not empirically good or bad. It depends on the underlying communication goals of a design, and on the users a design concept serves and supports. Creating content without an understanding of those goals, and of the narrative structure of the interface (whether synchronous and linear or otherwise), leads to many wasted words in a design.

Meeting the user's expectations

In any interface, providing the right amount of context at the right time is essential for setting expectations—which is vital if you want your users to progress. This doesn't mean explaining everything up front. It means setting up certain parameters so users have a framework for what's to follow.

All communication succeeds or fails by how it's received, not how it's stated. As well as understanding what content a design requires to communicate well, you must also understand how those words will be received—not just understood, but felt—by the user. Understanding the user's response will affect two things:

- The patterns of language you choose, at the level of parts of speech
- The style and expressiveness of your communication

The stylistic aspects of language—a product's style and tone—are also about expression. Typically, they are considered the final editorial layer of a product. They're the pixel-specific finish, akin to the choice of color or font.

Just like those choices, style and tone are heightened when they're woven deep into the fabric of the content itself. If you have a metaphor that underpins your primary concept and a label or name that fits your concept and product well, and you've architected your narrative in a particular way, then the stylistic choices available to you will start to emerge from that canvas. Especially if your content specialist has been involved throughout the process of clear concept definition, structure, and articulation, the style they apply will evolve naturally from those earlier choices.

This connectedness is what makes a product feel organic. It's the difference between thinking of style as a mere matter of copywriting and seeing it as the final step in making ideas concrete. And it goes beyond the text. In a finished artifact, the visual and the textual must exist in balance. You may choose to express certain ideas using color or iconography, and not text alone, or even remove text altogether from certain elements. Those semiotic choices are part of the product's style. Style is visual as well as verbal.

When pattern creation does come down to the text itself, there is an approach to style that requires a deep understanding not just of the concept and structure of a product, but of its users as well. Style isn't generated internally and pushed outward. It's not really about brand expression. It's about making space for empathy with the end user at the level of syntax, to show them that their needs are understood. A product doesn't always need to exactly mirror its audience's language, but it should be aware of it.

Reading your interface aloud (or hearing it read through a screen reader) is a great litmus test for this. It's entirely natural for us to fall back on cliché, ubiquitous phrases, and filler, created simply because the interface has enough space for them.

When this happens, we tend to overexplain the interface rather than letting the other tools of design do their work. Text itself has a role other than simple communication. In an interface, it also works as an interactive doorway that makes it clear what will happen when you click on a given term or phrase.

Where text meets the user

Text is made of small parts—words and phrases—that can be remixed in different combinations. You can think of these as modules of communication, sort of like Lego bricks. In modular nomenclature, a name can move through contexts and be transformed while still clearly expressing a well-defined concept (see Chapter 3).

Sentences are modular, too. They can be put together like the elements of a visual design, and they follow distinct patterns, just as visual elements do. By paying as much attention to language patterns as to interaction and visual patterns, you can find a deeper understanding of what is being communicated in a design.

The parts of a sentence can be manipulated to achieve different communication effects. By tuning in to communication at the sentence level and analyzing your text, you can get closer to what your design is trying to say and whether it's saying it coherently. You can do this just as you might look to design patterns to give your design visual unity.

Analyzing the elements of text in an interface can tell you different things about a design. First, it can tell you *why* certain text is able to communicate a message to a user, so that you can repeat the same pattern elsewhere to get the same result. Second, looking at text as a visual element helps integrate content with the design itself. In other words:

- **Parsing the structure of phrases** can tell you not just what's being communicated, but also which parts of speech are doing the most work in communicating to users. Just as auditing nouns and verbs across a system helps evaluate information architecture and nomenclature, in an individual screen or sequence, understanding how the parts of speech are working helps clarify what is being communicated. It allows you to turn text from subject copy into a repeatable, reliable communication system.
- **Looking at text as a visual element** means analyzing how text can be used within different visual patterns. For example, list items should follow a consistent pattern, while para-

graph text benefits from variation. The amount of space words take up in an interface contributes to the overall *gestalt* of the design.

This approach to sentence structure crops up in interface writing of all kinds. A very simple example of it in action is in an interface that's almost entirely made of writing: a chatbot.

Designing a conversation

When I was designing a chatbot for Intercom, I had to make some language decisions about this bot, and the team and I embarked on some research to analyze what was first thought of as the bot's tone of voice.

I knew that I wanted to go beyond tone and personality. A bot was almost entirely conversation, so I wanted to see how language choices worked at the level of parts of speech, and how those parts of speech met or missed the expectations of users. Only then, I felt, could I write a bot script—half of a conversation—founded on something systematic and objective that went beyond copywriting style.

A bot's personality is expressed entirely through text. So I needed to understand which pieces of text contributed to its personality and how they did so. Which pieces of bot communication were variable, and which formed the foundations of how users understood and interpreted it? To determine this, I worked with a researcher on a research plan that tested various versions of text. Each version varied the bot's speech within the following parameters:

- **Name variations:** We tested the terms "virtual assistant," "digital assistant," "bot," and other options for what we would call the tool, based on the company name. We also tested a version with no name at all.
- **Greetings:** We varied the introductions the chatbot would use to greet the user ("Hi, I'm [company name]'s digital assistant"). We tested a chirpy, friendly tone and a very neutral one, in combination with the various name sets.

- **Personal pronouns:** We tested whether the chatbot would use pronouns like "I," "we," and "you" in conversation, including versions with different pronouns and without.

Among all the names, pronouns, and variations of personality, the message was clear: the best bot was the one with a neutral personality. By looking at the different parts of speech that were being communicated by the bot, rather than just varying the tone of the text, we could see that it was personhood—a name and a pronoun—rather than the personality born from tone of voice alone, that rubbed users the wrong way.

Why? Well, my theory then and now was that a personified bot—one that used a first-person singular pronoun (I) or even a first-person plural pronoun (we), and that had a proper name, no matter what that name was—was introducing itself as a character to be known. And the user's goal—and more than that, their expectation—was not to deal with getting to know an automated character. Their goal was to get a question answered by a business they were writing to. At best, they hoped to get a reply from a real person. When a bot intervened (even for good reason; for example, to capture their email address so they could get a reply to their question if they closed a tab), it foregrounded itself in their experience in a way that didn't align with their goals.

Granular linguistic tests of this sort can be revelatory. They expose what lies beneath the surface of the interaction itself and allow you to fine-tune your understanding of users' expectations.

On another occasion, I used a very old testing method to understand people's comprehension: *cloze testing*. Rather than separating the parts of speech in a piece of text, just one word in every six is removed to see if users can fill in the blanks—and what words they use to do so. In this case, I used the following real website copy about a mortgage product:

But you should make sure your _____ will allow you to make _____ monthly payments if _____ rates start to go back up.

Users assumed the missing words were all negative, even punitive. They feared the text was telling them that they would lose their mortgage, money, or livelihood. For this example:

- Nearly 90 percent (26/29) of respondents said: "make sure your *lender/bank* will allow you to make *up* payments if *interest* rates start to go back up."
- Only 10 percent (3/29) of respondents got it right: "make sure your *budget/income* will allow you to make *higher* payments if *interest* rates start to go back up.

In this example, neutral advice was misinterpreted as a negative penalty, based on the subject and tone of the message. Users will meet text communication with their own expectations and emotions every time.

In the case of the Intercom chatbot, the lessons we learned by analyzing language did not imply that bots in general should avoid personification or personality; many examples (like Apple's Siri and Google's Alexa) show us otherwise. For this project, though, the bot needed a very toned-down persona, simply because of the construct in which it lived. It was a tool within a messaging system designed for people to speak to one another—not an intentional human-to-bot framework at all. Had the job been to design an app entirely built on an algorithm, where the prospect of speaking to a bot was not just expected but welcomed (however cautiously), the outcome could have been different.

As it was, our research findings informed many further executions of the system-level chatbot built by Intercom in that era. (Later, they opened their platform up for businesses to write their own bot scripts, which changed the underlying concept of the tool and what it did within the system.)

While simple, a chatbot is a singularly difficult design to master because it confines the user to a linear experience and often leaves them feeling disempowered. Understanding a bot (or any design) in terms of the parts of speech it uses to communicate can be a powerful window into users' comprehension of, and reaction to, the actual experience.

COMMUNICATING WITH VISUAL PATTERNS

Text is a visual element. Type size and weight, and how text elements are grouped, are fundamental tools of design. Hierarchy, proximity, the way text inhabits white space—all of these are visual decisions, and they convey meaning separate from the content that text creates.

Complex visual patterns also communicate meaning, in this case by creating a visual language or narrative across a product. Today, the bread and butter of design—choosing visual elements, laying out a screen—is often handled in part by a design system, or at least a shared user interface kit. Tools like these let large teams of designers apply components consistently, which reduces unintentional visual variation in a product.

A key word here is *unintentional*. Design systems are a wonderful solution for products that have a million color variations, because each designer chooses a slightly different gray for their drop shadows, or variations of simple components like check boxes, calls to action, or radio buttons.

What a design system can't do is communicate the goals of a design to the user. It can't generate a finished design any more than a font tool kit can write your content for you.

Design teams rely on design systems, but they can also feel hampered by them. What happens when a designer feels constrained like this? How can they determine when a case can be made for breaking with the system and making something new?

Principles before systems

Another element that should come before the finished design is a clear set of principles. In effect, the order of delivery for visual patterns should be as follows:

1. Problem
2. Concept
3. Principle
4. Pattern
5. Experience

Every design challenge starts with a clearly stated problem—but that problem can be answered by many different concepts. Once a concept is clearly defined, the desire to rush to visual patterns is strong. But the bridge from concept to the right design patterns and components must come not from visually matching components—thinking *I need some kind of modal, and here is the set of modals available for me to use*—but from the first principles you are working from when you design.

Many design projects start by establishing principles. One set of principles might be: effortless, insightful, attentive, and humble. We hope these principles will provide a connection to truth that will mitigate tendencies toward rote design or mimicry. We hope they'll keep us focused on why we're designing what we're designing.

For a long time, I believed that a strong principle was one that had a strong opposing argument—that any starting point worth starting from, an opinionated principle, had to be something you could argue just as well against. This felt right, because a principle that was too obvious was just a truism, something everyone already believed. How would that help you make a strong decision when faced with two or more possible design directions to take?

I no longer think a binary approach to principles is enough. If you've ever tried to directly apply a set of principles to a product decision, you know they don't cover all eventualities. It's easy to create principles that are opinionated without providing real direction. Looking for something spiky isn't always going to lead you to focus on the actual need you're designing for, and therefore won't always lead you down the most direct path to success. Sometimes it's best to see what practical decisions need to be made about a product and work back from there, making principles more an act of deducing what feels right rather than imposing hard constraints.

A principle is a means of aiming a group of people in the same direction, with clarity. It should act like a compass that brings you back to a path when you stray from it. There is nothing within the word "principle" that says it must be debatable. If you are on a journey in search of water and smell salt in the air, no one would argue that you should go in the opposite direction. Sometimes the obvious thing is absolutely the right thing to do.

Evaluating principles based on how debatable or contentious they are won't always lead to great design decisions, because it's possible to care more about the opinion and the debate it inspires than about the outcome.

A principle should try to inspire as well as tie back to a clear conceptual goal. It should both teach and clarify, and make the resulting design better.

Patterns and systems

A principle will help design teams evaluate the success of a design. It won't do the work for them. Patterns must be evaluated based on how well they tell the story of a concept—how well they communicate.

Every communication effort in a product has many elements that are shared—nomenclature, rhythm, style—but every experience also differs from its neighbors in nuanced ways. This means that patterns must be applied critically, and they must be considered as aspects of an entire experience.

The pitfalls of design systems

Many designers work in design teams hundreds of people strong. Design systems help teams keep large numbers of design decisions on a more even keel. But these systems can kill the natural authorship that every designer should feel over what they are designing and the users they design for.

The way users experience a product that has a consistent design system—consistent patterns—may not be the way the makers of the design system see those patterns. Imagine a deck of cards, laid out on a table, organized by suit and number (FIG 5.7).

This is how designers see patterns, as designers using a design system—designers are the dealers, and we see the whole deck of cards. We should know each card fits into a group and has rules about how it should be used. It's easy for us to have no opinion about how and where it shows up. Patterns can be

FIG 5.7: These vintage playing cards are beautiful as a set, but also make sense when viewed individually.

seen as a set of tools that will contribute to overall consistency, whatever game we play.

Cards are experienced differently if you're the person on the other side of the card table, playing the game—you see the patterns of suit and number, but only as they appear in the gameplay you're experiencing. This is how users of our products encounter patterns: as part of a narrative.

Users of a product will try to make their way through it to achieve their goal, *even if* no one had gone to the effort of organizing the pieces of the pathway into consistent patterns. The consistencies we offer can help them find their way and, most of all, help them discover other paths in the future. Consistency's greatest advantage is that it helps users learn. It's like showing someone the rules of play so they can learn future pathways more easily.

But consistency alone doesn't make for great design. Design systems applied in a rote fashion can lead us to build from components without really thinking about the coherence of our completed designs. Because we're using the "right" component, we might think the finished product will be correct and coherent.

Incoherent design can look like using a pattern in the wrong context, or—which is more common, and harder to fix—paying attention only to the component and not the whole screen, flow, or experience. Even when a design component is updated, often it is updated in isolation, removed from the context of a page. This means its changes will not make sense for every application.

Design systems present a huge advantage for product teams, but when they're not governed correctly or used critically, they can limit your choices. Their architects often don't intend this, but a system can create distance between the designer and what they're trying to communicate. Watch out for rote use of design system patterns. A good test for this is to make sure you can make a case for the design of an entire screen, even if you're adding a single element. If you find yourself thinking only of the element you need to add, and making the argument that you should use a given component "because it's from the system," take a step back and consider the experience holistically. A design is a complete thing, not just its parts, and it should be considered as a single unit.

Patterns must be used with both a system awareness and screen-level focus on the story they are being used to tell. If that work isn't done, products begin to look not like an artful, modular structure but like a poorly made, prefabricated house.

And poor use of design systems is a problem that compounds. Rules are no good to us when we follow them without closely examining them. Instead, aim to understand a design problem on its own terms first, before seeing what patterns might support it. That means digging into each of the themes already discussed, even if you're being encouraged to design something that deliberately copies something else. When we begin to assemble a solution from Lego pieces that already exist without doing the work of understanding our idea deeply and defining it clearly, we won't gain the understanding necessary to challenge and evolve a system.

Always be editing (the design system)

Perhaps the best design system is one that is less opinionated about structure and more opinionated about style. Colleagues who work on Polaris, the Shopify design system, often make a

FIG 5.8: A simple component contains only the elements it needs to be complete. It does not presuppose its intended context.

distinction between using the system to inform a design decision and designing the system itself.

Designer José Torre has written about this, noting that "pages in our experience felt like they weren't specifically designed for a problem. Instead, they rely on established templates […] that are fairly generic, but aren't always the best solution to a unique problem" (https://bkaprt.com/dd46/05-01).

Design systems must not become too rigid. That rigidity can often come from an information architecture decision about the system itself: how complex its components are.

A simple design component is more like an element, or an atom—for example, a specific heading style or an individual checkbox (FIG 5.8). Its job is to provide visual consistency, but not to define *how it might be used* in combination with other elements. This turns the system into a set of very small parts that can be broken down and remixed by the designer closest to the problem being solved and the concept being communicated.

Complex components, on the other hand, combine many elements together in ways that can feel fixed (FIG 5.9). A modal component with many available text elements will often get filled with unnecessary content because to remove those elements feels like a break with the system, rather than the natural and correct choice about which elements need to be included to clearly communicate an idea.

Even the simple arrangement of elements in a field label pattern can occasionally be overly complex. For example, field labels sometimes contain additional elements that are not relevant, such as the addition of "Help text," which implies that

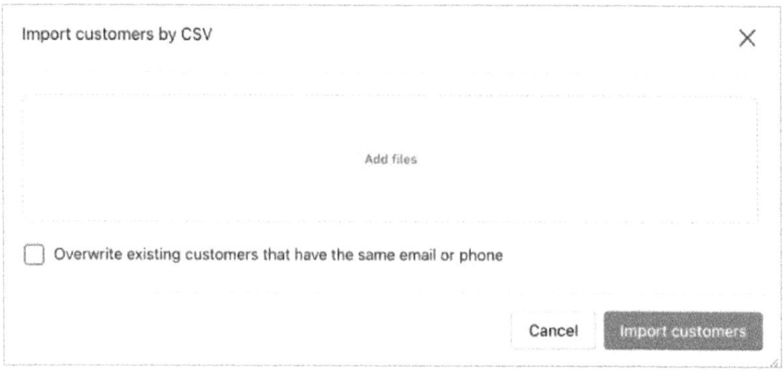

FIG 5.9: A complex component may contain too many elements, some of which need to be removed to clarify the message. For example, the checkbox beneath this file-import pattern provides a safeguard that may not always be required if it's used for less risky file types.

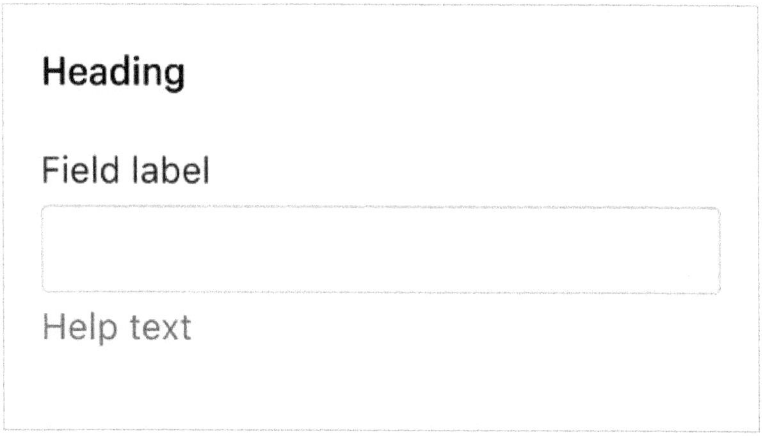

FIG 5.10: A relatively simple component can still be too complex for a design's needs. Here, "Help text" is included but not necessary.

help text must be included when in fact it might not be needed (**FIG 5.10**).

Most design systems are not *intended* to lock designers into one way of doing things, but merely to provide parameters to work within and even push against. "A floor, not a ceiling" is how people usually say Shopify's Polaris design system should be used—and this slightly confusing framing (a rule book one must sometimes ignore) is not unique to Polaris. Most sets of design principles convey similar ideas. But in practice, design system rule books, much like dictionaries, get quoted verbatim. So designs simply fill the space the system provides rather than using system components in innovative ways, or challenging them outright as often as they should.

Just like parsing text to get at the parts of speech that really communicate an idea to a user, design systems must be interrogated so that only the pieces that are really required make it into the finished experience. What results is a visually coherent, lean, and focused design that puts the user's comprehension of the concept above all other concerns.

GETTING OUT OF YOUR OWN WAY

The final stage of design, when we are *making the thing*, can be the stage that's more prone to stumbling blocks than any other. The closer we are to an experience we're making, the more we begin to identify with certain approaches and get attached to them.

It's easy to start making quick assumptions—about what we need to say and how best to present it. Even with the most open-minded approach and the best will in the world, we're all human and we all bring our biases to the table. We're hardwired that way. The idea of a designer as an empty vessel with no opinions of their own is as damaging an image of design's role as the stereotype of the design expert who knows all.

The assumptions closest to our own experience are the hardest to unseat, which is why making space to explore those assumptions is important. The refrain "we're all speaking a different language" is a sign that those involved in a design should dig into what each of them thinks they are making. So many missed connections in projects come from a failure to challenge these assumptions.

Challenging our own assumptions and mental models strengthens the muscles of critical thinking and self-analysis we all need when we design. As with everything in user experience design, the purpose is to remember that you're not designing for yourself, and to try to see the world through another person's eyes. Doing this consistently takes effort, focus, and a reminder of the real role of design: to facilitate the transfer of meaning.

6 WHEN WORDS CHANGE

WRITING IS A PROCESS OF DISCOVERY. Even the writing of this book was a process of discovering what I'd been thinking about over a decade and a half of working on digital websites and products. I was defining concepts long before I realized that it was the fundamental truth of my role—that my job was to describe and clarify the ideas that could become things, rather than just writing the words that appeared *in* those things.

Thinking about concepts in this way has also helped me step back and understand naming as a process projects go through, rather than as a point of arrival. When we design something, attach names to it, and create a visual representation of it, it feels like we've created a space in the world—because we have. As a product evolves, we begin building new rooms onto that space until it starts to become ungainly: an architectural oddity.

These changes are easy to spot once you start looking for them. A product that doesn't evolve tends to contain terminology that doesn't make sense to its users. Rather than revise its design and content, such a product pays for this lack of user understanding with more support calls and help documentation.

Products that recognize when change is needed tend to adopt new design paradigms, new names, and new ways of telling their story. They relaunch themselves when the time is right and go after new types of users with designs and concepts that are customized for those markets. This is healthy, and great for users when done well, but can be earthshakingly difficult for the designers (and engineers, product managers, and everyone else) making the product, who have always known a concept or feature in a certain way and have talked about it using specific frameworks and terminology.

How firmly should teams hold on to existing frameworks and language? How much evolution is the right amount, and how can we recognize it when it's approaching? The first step is simply to embrace the possibility and promise of change. Like new words in a dictionary, change is a sign that a product is thriving.

Some products evolve to the point where a concept or feature branches off in a new direction entirely. When that happens, the concept can require an entirely new design, new name, and new framework, not just a few new or tweaked elements. I've seen this happen in my work in product concepts like chatbots, around design patterns like overlays and modals, and in industry fundamentals like the definition of "platform." There is always an argument to be had, always someone's mental model that needs to be contended with. The work of design is also the work of argument.

HOW IDEAS CHANGE

When you design a chair, it stays a chair. When you design a new home, you can define the key parts that go into that building; once created, they're relatively immovable (renovations notwithstanding). In addition, the character of the home—its architectural style and details—will inform any future change you might make (unless it falls victim to an unsympathetic developer).

With a building, you have created a real-world representation of an idea, and while it might inspire new ideas, the original representation stays the same. This may be why we see ideas come back around again in so many forms of physical design—in architecture, in fashion, in furniture. The original objects are there as a constant source of inspiration, to be riffed on and reexamined.

In a digital system, very few parts are truly load-bearing and unchangeable. The whole system can be reimagined, and this change can happen at a rapid pace. Perhaps that's why there is such a drive to look forward rather than back in digital design.

Design in digital spaces is likely to evolve toward new tools, whether that means the virtual reality paradigms of a metaverse or something currently unconceived. We have always adapted to text and to surfaces. In fact, both text and surfaces are fundamental to most examples of written text. A surface separates the person reading from the thing they are reading or interacting with. And those last few words are key. There is a difference between information consumption and immersion. Console and many online games are immersive, but they are linear narratives in visual space. The internet, though, with its separation of content from the person viewing that content, can be traversed in many directions without any immersive quality at all—perhaps better for fact-finding and task-completing use cases.

Games and movies also rely on precise scripts, game rules, stories, and story mechanics. Productivity tools used on screens rely on two-dimensional containers and the *classification* of concepts in those containers—folders, and labels on folders. The labels define what is in each folder; for the folders to change, so must the labels.

Concepts need to shift intentionally, and often drift unintentionally, for three reasons:

- **They have a loose grip on their own history.** Technology is inherently ephemeral, in a way that makes it hard for it to reflect on its own history.
- **They can be visualized in ways that aren't as limited by concrete reality.** Technology products exist in invented space. The problems they solve can be deconstructed and solved in new ways.
- **They rely on words as their foundation.** Technology products are fundamentally linguistic. As new ideas are added or

new problems appear that need solving, the linguistic classifications that drive them may just not be enough anymore.

Change is inevitable in product design. Understanding a change's point of origin, who can best manage it, and who benefits from it, can help you navigate it with less frustration and more imagination.

When to change

Technology companies are machines for meaning. Sometimes that meaning isn't clearly thought through, but the fact is that as designers, it's our job to think it through—to define things in terms and in interfaces.

When I first joined Intercom, its products were named after the job they did for the user. For example, the job of responding to support conversations was housed in a product called "Respond," while the tool for creating marketing outreach emails was called "Engage." But it became clear that potential customers struggled to identify with these names, and the company had to grapple with a product rebrand. This type of change ricochets across the design of an entire product and can represent tremendous overhead for design teams, justified as the changes might be.

It's curious that we can be resistant to change when we work in a medium designed for it. But we can get better at dealing with—and even welcoming—real, meaningful product evolution by watching out for some of its more noticeable triggers and causes:

- The product or design has stagnated, and a pivot is required.
- A new technology or innovation (or perhaps competition) may make change not only desirable, but unavoidable. The old way of doing things doesn't make sense to the customers you want to serve. You're approaching a true rebranding.
- A company may have evolved its goals, or its customers may have changed.
- Growth may have come quickly but wildly, and the product might need to step back and communicate clearer goals.

- Designers are often the bellwethers for when things stop making sense. They see that it's become harder to build new things, or that consistency and clarity are harder to achieve, despite their best efforts.

When a product asks its users to relearn something, there's a cognitive cost to the user that can be frustrating. That means there are also costs to the business when frustrated users call or contact its support team in greater numbers. Because the user's mental model is something they bring with them, they carry along terms they learn from other products, even if the new concept and interface design is simpler and better.

Even when features are just renamed, the product develops a burn list. Words that used to mean one thing can't easily morph into a new thing. Better to introduce an entirely new word than to borrow from somewhere else.

Who makes the change?

Change happens to products and companies no matter who's involved. But a concept shift can either happen *to* you, or you can be involved in how it happens.

Content designers and other writing or language specialists can be very effective at identifying the need for change, especially when it comes to nomenclature. Whether a change is needed in a name alone, or in a concept or an entire system, people primed to consider words can bring storytelling, pattern-finding, and sense-making skills to the table to help gauge the size and scale of the change needed. As a content designer myself, I have always seen my job as one of holding a mirror up to the products being built, by solving problems of semantics, meaning, and organization.

If you don't have language specialists on board, the work of guiding language or informational or system change can still be done effectively and intentionally. It simply requires taking the time to consider the patterns, themes, metaphors, and structures at play in your product.

User-driven change

While doing the work of analyzing the concepts in a product, you constantly need to look outward toward the users of the product you're designing—not only to keep that audience front and center in your mind, but to be aware of any subtle current of change that could affect the design and concept.

Ideas and concepts often change because users change. This happens slowly, and it can be hard to pinpoint when a concept has outgrown its casing—whether its name, design, or entire reason for existing is in question. Sometimes a feature was never very logical, but it was created when a platform was in its infancy, and those who've lived with it have become inured to its lack of logic. Even users and long-standing employees have become used to it.

Happily, there's a great litmus test built into almost every company: new employees. When a new designer starts examining a feature, they can shine a useful—if uncomfortable—light on concepts that no longer make sense.

A more appropriate framing

When starting a company, a common aim is to create a *minimum viable product* (MVP). That often requires focusing on a few very specific needs and a specific subset of potential customers. A company in its earliest stages that is focused on finding product market fit will naturally choose names and language that define that market and those potential customers. And those language choices will organically tell a story about what that product is and whom it is for.

I experienced this at Intercom when I advised on a change to a core concept. When I joined the company, they referred to all users as "admins." This was appropriate when the company was first founded. It was initially designed for small teams of a few people; in that world, everyone really *was* an admin. Four years later, that was no longer true. Team collaboration was a huge theme of the company's story. It had a product called a "team inbox" and concepts like "assignment rules" that helped people share work in real time. I advised changing this primary user definition to "teammate" to reflect the collaborative nature of the audience they were building for.

Listening to users' language

Sometimes, users themselves will suggest a change in language or structure, even without realizing it. For example, I spoke to an engineer for a platform that offers funding and planning tools to charitable or social-good organizations. When they first conceived of the platform, they had to describe their users and how those users should manage their work on the platform.

At the start, they assumed their users would be small, local charitable groups just getting off the ground. So they chose the word "starters" to describe those asking for funding, and "location" as the fundamental way starters would organize.

Eventually, the company realized this didn't reflect reality. Some people asking for funding worked in established organizations, so "starters" wasn't an accurate name. It described only that they were at the "start" of their association with the platform—which was not a meaningful attribute they'd use to describe themselves. And with the spread of remote fundraising, more organizations ignored both regional and national boundaries. Users referred to their organizations simply as "groups," and even called the locations page in the product—which was literally labeled "Locations"—the "groups" page.

As with the Intercom "teammates" example, this change was a good thing. The utility of the product, and the variety of its user base, had stretched beyond the company's original concept of itself. The company's designers and engineers had to change their language to fit that new scope.

The impact of fundamental name changes

Some of these changes might seem like simple name changes on the surface, but their roots go deeper. The way a company describes its users is a fundamental part of the story of a platform. So if the way that story is expressed is out of step with those users' reality, a natural but sometimes hard-to-detect tension arises.

This can affect how designers, product managers, and engineers building a product communicate with one another. In a poorly named or structured system where ambiguity exists around names or information architecture, team members and stakeholders often need to communicate twice—first to clarify which feature or topic they're talking about, and then to clarify the issue or improvement they're discussing. This is needlessly wasteful, and far more common than it should be.

When a name that's present in a product's architecture changes, it can mean more than changing an interface label; it might also mean making changes to the code itself. When designers for the social-good platform changed the product's terminology around "starters" and "locations," they opted not to update its code base, but ensured that the new terminology was referenced in technical documents. Once the engineers had gone to the effort of cleaning up their language, everybody else on the team did, too.

There's huge value in having clarity around the objects in the code and the naming in the code, but it's often not appropriate to aim to have the same language from code to customer. At the same time, it helps when there is some root relationship between the coded term and the interface term. The two types of terms may need to be distinct for the product to evolve, but there should nevertheless be a relationship between them.

If a story can tune in to the language and narrative that exists in users' minds and genuinely reflect how a company plans to serve those users, there's an additional benefit. The company can start to more closely echo its users' language and vocabulary, because it will now be telling the same story about users that users tell about themselves.

Changes of scale and context

Sometimes you evolve a name because your audience is not responding to it from its context, or simply doesn't understand what it does. What's harder to gauge, but is just as common, is when the scope of the problem it solves has broadened or changed. The job to be done is slightly different than it was.

For example, a swiping interaction feels core to how dating apps work on mobile devices, but it could evolve into a completely different interaction. Sometimes the step forward technologically will be enough to push you to change a name—imagine what interaction details and feature names might exist in a metaverse dating context! The point is that patenting names that are highly descriptive is problematic, not just for other apps that also make use of that interaction, but because it could date your feature by tying it to a particular device.

Despite this natural evolution, apps *do* patent common interactions. In the case of Bumble, many of its competitor dating apps also contain versions of the word "swipe" with certain capitalization patterns. The Bumble team had to be very careful about adopting those patterns.

The team also had to stay mindful of the need to future-proof even gestural norms, like swiping. Candi Williams, Bumble's head of content design, pointed out that while these norms are ubiquitous today, they might not always be. Who knows what the future will bring?

Features also need some room to accommodate different emotional scenarios. The Bumble team, Williams continued, was careful to avoid language that was descriptive. For example, a friendly "Share your date" prompt would feel inappropriate if a user wanted to share details of their date for safety reasons.

The team also paid close attention to accessibility. For example, the act of "swiping" is inaccessible to users who don't use gestures to navigate through the app. Bumble has so many users using the app in different ways, Williams said, that if a design approach excludes one in a hundred people and there's a reasonable inclusive alternative, they will use the alternative.

DESIGN SYSTEMS AND CHANGE

Design systems serve conflicting purposes. They can allow teams to build coherent designs more quickly, for example. But fixed design systems can also hold a product in place. A system that doesn't change will become visually stagnant.

In the excitement over efficiency, it's easy to forget that the value of a design system is to make it easier to develop, and this need requires that teams feed new information into it all the time—not just because they've seen new design trends they want to follow, but because they've learned something about how people use the product that pushes them toward change. Healthy teams look outward to see what usage tells them about the system.

A well-curated design system can solve problems of consistency, but if consistency is the only purpose of a design system, it can become a hindrance to good design. This can happen when:

- Patterns that look similar have very different purposes (or vice versa)
- Teams tend to stick with an existing pattern even if it's substandard, leading to stagnant and dated experiences

Similar, but different

When we conflate patterns with one another—to look only at similarities in visual terms and not in terms of utility, in terms of what a pattern is for—there can be an attempt, most damagingly, to look for consistency in the wrong corners.

In the exploration of Shopify's overlay patterns (see Chapter 5), the turning point was realizing that our team wasn't just debating the right pattern for a specific stage in the narrative through the product. We were also debating design-pattern consistency, asking ourselves: "How many overlay patterns do we need? How many is too many?"

Overlay patterns are useful in browser-based apps because they allow you to carry out a workflow without traversing an entire app and refreshing the page every time. They allow a browser-based experience to feel more like an operating system or desktop app experience. We debated the value of overlays that took up the full width of the browser. The Shopify design system already contained full-screen designs that let users edit content or data. Why not consider using the same pattern for this new settings section?

FIG 6.1: In an operating system like MacOS, self-contained windows layer on top of one another.

To justify the existence of this new pattern, we needed to consider two questions:

- What purpose did the new pattern serve?
- Was it important to limit the number of overlay patterns in the system?

While evaluating the new pattern, we looked at comparisons outside our system. Operating systems use the pattern of the *sheet*—a full-screen layer—as a foundation of the OS interface. Operating systems can't work without sheets, which let the user switch between apps across a system, act as containers for each app, and help users understand the space of the system (**FIG 6.1**).

In a browser app like ours, the sheet pattern wasn't as vitally necessary. The app could function without it. And we already had a bunch of different "sheet" styles for different types of content. Ultimately, we did create a new pattern variation that fit our content and our goals; the new pattern was based on the

FIG 6.2: The new drawer pattern, still attached to the browser tab below it, offers a peek of that tab at the top.

concept of a "drawer" rather than a "container" and couldn't be detached from the browser below it (**FIG 6.2**).

There was perhaps no right answer here. But the process of going through this internal debate helped us understand some deep things—like how close we wanted to push our design toward non-browser-based patterns. And it also helped us unearth many *unnecessary* variations we already had in the various modals in our system. Even if we had decided to stick with our existing patterns, the debate would have been worthwhile, because it would have told us something meaningful about the direction we wanted our design language to take.

Quality and speed

Quality is a tough concept to measure, especially when it comes to design interfaces. It's something all designers reach for, but it can be very hard to define. At Shopify, we defined it in a few different pillars, including a feature's usability, its aesthetics, and its adherence to business strategy.

In my experience, though, what sets apart a high-quality decision from a mediocre design solution can be a matter of taste. Taste can be a polarizing word when it's taken out of context—and taste *needs* context.

To me, taste is the sense of what "feels right" in a given situation. To apply it, you need to have a very strong sense of the house style you're designing within. And that means the product you're designing needs to have a very well-defined sensibility. Think of it as cuisine. Many foods taste good, but we might not all be able to tell which flavors feel appropriate to a certain style of cuisine. The balance of flavors, textures, and aromas all connect to the sensibility of any kind of food, whether it's high cuisine or poutine (yes, there's a quality bar for cheese curds and gravy). And to apply taste, we need a common understanding of what "good" looks like for the kind of dish we're trying to make.

At Shopify, we formed a team that was specifically focused on design quality. We realized we were always deprioritizing work that was focused on taste and on raising the bar for the kind of product we wanted. The design system we had could not do this job for us, because that wasn't its job. The design system was a tool for making our design consistent, rather than a tool for highlighting and focusing in on simple improvements that, in aggregate, could make the entire product a little bit better, week by week and day by day.

This design-quality team focused on the small details that make the product better in focused ways, rather than on improving everything at the component level (FIG 6.3). The team has been successful for three reasons:

- It focuses on making things better, not perfect.
- It focuses on making things better *in the style we're aiming for.*
- It focuses on doing a lot of small things very quickly.

While the design system is designed to slowly integrate improvements and smooth out inconsistencies over time, the quality team's focus is on fixing specific tiny details very fast,

FIG 6.3: Delivering small improvements—like this revision of a search empty state—helps make a product feel more considered.

and only later having those changes get absorbed into smoothed-out component updates in the system. The two teams, like a nerve ending and a brain, work together symbiotically.

MAJOR REDESIGNS AND NEW APPROACHES

Occasionally, a product must be rethought from the platform level up. One way this can manifest is in a need for greater personalization or customization for users. This often happens because the users of a product have more complex needs that can't be served by an experience that's the same for everyone. This is particularly true in business-to-business products, especially when they start to serve enterprise customers. Customization of this kind is often unnecessary in smaller products built for customers with less complex needs.

This desire for change can lead teams toward a desire to adapt an entire product, sometimes drastically. And this in turn can lead to new interfaces and new ways of selling a product offering. It can also lead to changes at the platform or API level—to customization of a product's fundamental concepts.

In my experience, product teams often avoid or stave off customization for a few reasons:

- They're aiming for simplicity. Complex products are harder to maintain and more difficult to design iteratively.
- They believe a customized product is inherently unopinionated about how it should be used. They might feel the need to be opinionated about the elements a product should or should not include.

Many small products succeed in having a simple (and therefore good) design because they create smart defaults for users to work with, or because they even limit outright what users should do. A former design director of mine used to advise that products should ideally have no settings at all, because configuration is too much of a chore.

But as companies grow and their customers become more complex, assumptions about what users need should be challenged. A good design for a more complex customer is most often not a minimalist design with few controls (though this is not a hard and fast rule).

A great example of our contradictory assumptions about complexity can be found in our own design tools. While we often aim to remove detailed controls from the tools we design, our tools—whether Figma, Sketch, or Photoshop—offer an array of control and flexibility. Figma, for example, was created to offer designers complete control over their design artifacts (FIG 6.4).

As designers, we must fight against the tendency to believe we always know what's best. We must consciously scale our ideas in pace with our customers' needs. If your product sustains itself, its typical user will change. These new, larger customers need more flexibility to adapt to their specific needs, and eventually their frustrations must be assuaged by adding some of that flexibility to the product.

Complex needs should not be equated with heavy-handed or ugly design solutions. These shifting needs simply require that the tools designed for them be scalable. Different platforms handle the need for flexibility in different ways. For example, Google's enterprise products feel very aligned with its consumer experiences, and it intentionally hides some of its com-

FIG 6.4: This example of a Figma pattern set illustrates the granular control designers have over their artifacts.

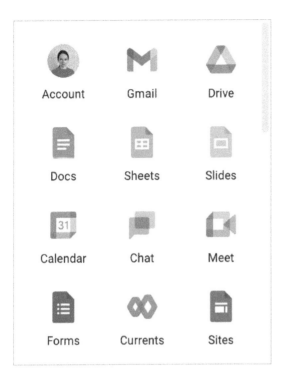

FIG 6.5: Google's Enterprise product suite looks indistinguishable from its consumer products at this level.

plexity and configuration—in an often arcane and complex information architecture, it must be said (**FIG 6.5**).

Whatever design direction a platform takes as it grows along with its customers, you should ask two fundamental questions as you take on more conceptual complexity and more bespoke user needs: Where does that complexity live in your product, and how can it be moved around?

One driver of these decisions might be whether there's an evolving role in your customers' companies that's dedicated to your platform. It may become someone's job to set up and manage what you design. That doesn't mean making their job harder, but it does mean being careful about taking tools out of their hands.

Larger companies also like to put their own stamp on the technology they use. They like to configure colors and logos so that the software they're paying for feels like theirs. They want external software to be seamless with their own software tools.

Moving this complexity around and dealing with fundamental changes in customer needs isn't a straightforward process. And it'll be easier to change some things—such as product names, marketing, or packaging—before changing the product architecture itself.

A CULTURE OF CHANGE

As companies grow, even the best of them can get fuzzy around the edges. The best ideas do not always make their way through to fruitful outcomes, and the best design decisions can become drowned in a sea of stakeholders. This doesn't happen because people want unclear outcomes, or even because they don't value good design. It happens mostly because communication is universally hard. (Counterintuitively, embracing this fact helps us understand each other better).

Communication can break down in a few ways, but perhaps the largest generator of fuzzy thinking is the existence of hierarchy. Companies tend to be hierarchical, so there is always a power imbalance. The mere existence of power creates that imbalance. So much of our time in corporations is spent evaluating our distance from the proverbial seat at the table, or from the next rung on the ladder. It can be nigh impossible to create space for real meaning and real exploration in such an environment.

Designers are often advised to embrace business needs, and to understand the numbers and goals those needs impose. A company's goals are vital to understand, of course. They're why you're making your product in the first place, and they should help you aim at the right thing. But business goals alone can't make a design work. The primary responsibility of design is to argue for and transfer *meaning*.

Focusing too intently on business needs—especially when divorced from context or balanced discussion of meaning and user understanding—risks drowning out valid avenues of exploration, either because of poor communication or poor translation of priorities. The irony is that by focusing on business impact alone, you might disregard avenues of design exploration that aren't *ipso facto* bad business ideas—they might even be brilliant ones. They're just often the less obvious paths to take.

As designers, we also want to work on things that have a reality outside of the organization. We want to explore the needs of people we already design for, and find ways to design for new people, so we can uncover new problems and do new things. That means we seek out change—though we don't necessarily find it easy when it happens.

As companies grow, even as the development of new products accelerates, the desire to challenge fundamental definitions wanes because the cost of that change increases. Yet there are times when a conceptual pivot or a new metaphor is demonstrably worth the cost.

Change is an emotional process as well as a technical one. Taking the time to create clear concepts with your team, and developing a perspective on how your product might evolve as you do so, requires investment in a design culture where that evolution is expected, accepted, and encouraged—where it's something to be faced head-on, rather than something to sidle up to or panic about.

Creating a culture that embraces shifting concepts asks that you first consider the making of ideas and the definition of concepts to be a continuous part of the design process. When you make sure a whole team understands the world they're building toward, you unlock power for everyone. And when you get it right, your idea won't feel like a directive—it's a blueprint.

There are so many ways to start this process of defining concepts continuously and anticipating when they'll change:

- Often a design system starts as an audit of visual patterns, and so becomes a snapshot of that product's design at a particular point in time. Patterns might be vetted and improved, but only in terms of internal comparison and visual taste. Instead, imagine developing a design system starting not with patterns, but with metaphors and concepts. You might then think about how well your patterns represent the concepts you're trying to convey.

- Another way in is through user research. Try to pick up on the times when a concept, metaphor, or name doesn't make sense for your audience, or doesn't find its way into the language they use to talk about your product to you. In short, find self-awareness by taking the time to listen to how others describe you.
- Research your team's mental models. Understand how you all see the product differently, and treat it as a process of discovery, instead of an opportunity to get defensive about those differences.
- Create a glossary and make it public. Open source your words. So much of what we create in tech is not new, and we all benefit from shared definitions. Working in public helps everyone.

Synthesizing concepts and categorizing a system are storytelling, pattern-finding, sense-making skills. There are likely people on your team with these skills; they can hold up a mirror that reflects your product back to you.

Products are systems. Systems need to be clearly defined. Today, products designed to disrupt enterprise software succumb to the same dangers of feature bloat. It's difficult to keep the user front and center when defining a model for a product that's both flexible and long-lasting.

Be aware of the world a product lives in, and the concepts and metaphors that take shape around it—especially if your product is generating or, as is more common, co-opting some of those metaphors. Design is not set apart from the world; it's part of the world. Technology's desire to define the future can't come at the expense of knowing its role in, and influence on, the present.

Change will find your product no matter what happens, and no matter whether you're designing something that wants to be around in a century or just wants to live long enough to be bought and sold. Be ready for it. Embrace it.

Design through it.

CONCLUSION

❝ The worst thing one can do with words is surrender to them.
—GEORGE ORWELL (*POLITICS AND THE ENGLISH LANGUAGE*)

ORWELL WROTE THESE WORDS to remind us that language can hinder expression as much as help it. And language hinders us most when we fail to wield it with control, or when we push it to one side as though it were a detail of design rather than design's foundation.

Like images, sounds, shapes, and color, words are tools of thought. They convey context, nuance and meaning, but they're also hard to control. Language, as a communication tool, contradicts itself by making communication difficult. Yet we must grapple with it to create concepts that make sense.

Anytime you attempt to capture a concept, you must make sense of that concept to yourself before you can express it to anyone else. This sense-making process is ongoing, whether you're clarifying your own ideas or trying to convey what you mean to others.

This is especially true in product design, where designs are changeable and ephemeral. And it's especially necessary because of the way we get our ideas—often not fresh and new, but borrowed from other companies. We borrow entire products and sets of features, visual and interaction patterns, and even the fundamental parts of our systems. As we borrow those ideas, the words that define them come along for the ride.

Words are at the root of everything we design. You can use those shared roots with greater success by deepening the parts of your design practice that involve language and inviting in steps and methods that are new or little used. You might take more time to consider information architecture and taxonomy, or to more regularly research mental models (including your own). You might start thinking of metaphors to use to frame and name your products, or take more time—and enjoyment—in plotting out product narratives.

This care over concepts will serve you well when a product's names and stories wear out. This change is a good thing. It means people are responding to the work you've made and want it to *do* more, to be more powerful, to tell a bigger story. Rethinking your concepts need not feel like tearing down a building. Instead, it can feel like being ready to surf a wave that might bring you onto an unexpected shore.

The word *concept*, with its roots in *conception*, hints that the work of defining a concept is a process, one that asks for patience and attention. That process *is* the work of design: not merely a series of steps or guidelines to follow, but an act of clear thought.

ACKNOWLEDGMENTS

THANK YOU TO MY BRILLIANT, patient editors—Greg Nicholl, Caren Litherland, and Lisa Maria Marquis—as well as my early reader and last-minute editor, Katie Elder.

This book never would have come into being without Kristina Halvorson, who convinced me to submit an outline, and may not have been seen through to its end without Kate Towsey, as we wrote our first books together on opposite sides of the world.

I am enormously grateful to everyone who shared their experiences, resources, and drawings of sandwiches with me in the process of making this book: to Marta Masters, Chelsea Larsson, Emmet Connolly, Candi Williams, Amogh Sarda, Laura Murphy-Chalkin, Johan Stromqvist, Tarek Khalil, Sadie Redden, Owen Williams, Quentin Dietrich, Meredith Castile, and Dorian Taylor, thank you many times over for your insights.

My deepest thanks to Khoi Vinh for contributing his wonderful foreword and his editorial insight, and to Stewart Scott-Curran, Randall Snare, Peter Merholz, and Amy Thibodeau for their very generous blurbs.

I'd also like to thank my family: Katie, Angus, Euan, Sean, Antonia, and Abby; as well as my extended family and friends on both sides of the Atlantic.

RESOURCES

MANY OF MY OWN RESOURCES on writing were books already on my shelves and in my bookmarks, but I chanced across lots of other articles and materials that spoke to me, directly or indirectly, about the power of words to create meaning.

I found inspiration in places that were unexpected and perhaps not designed to speak to my topic organically—books about photography, or art, or mathematics. But these became my favorite wells to draw from. Creativity comes from the side paths and detours, rather than from direct instruction.

I hope that these resources, and any other pebbles you might pick up on your own road to thinking about language and meaning in design, will help you feel surefooted.

Concepts and creativity

Walter Benjamin, "The Work of Art in the Age of Mechanical Reproduction." This appeared in *Illuminations,* edited by Hannah Arendt and translated by Harry Zohn. Much of Berger's inspiration for *Ways of Seeing* came from this Benjamin essay, so you might prefer to go straight to the source (https://bkaprt.com/dd46/07-01, PDF).

John Berger, *Ways of Seeing.* A four-part BBC TV series that preceded this book, available for free on YouTube (https://bkaprt.com/dd46/07-02), preceded this book. Berger was an art critic concerned with the ways our modern eyes perceive the Western art canon. His topic is perspective, which I found relevant for thinking about the ways we perceive "reality" through words—and I was entranced by his way of seeing, "as though pictures were like words" (https://bkaprt.com/dd46/07-03/).

Kyna Leski, *The Storm of Creativity.* This is an arresting treatise on the creative process, and an argument that creativity and the creative process are universal and unbounded, "like a storm" that overtakes us in waves (https://bkaprt.com/dd46/07-04/).

Dieter Rams, *The Power of Good Design*. In 2018 and 2019, I had the pleasure of working with Vitsoe, the British producer of Rams's iconic furniture and shelving. I had heard of Rams's principles before then, but working surrounded by his designs was transformational—the essence of good design come to life (https://bkaprt.com/dd46/07-05/).

Semantics and logic

Willard van Orman Quine, *From a Logical Point of View*. Quine's premise in this group of essays is that we view the world through a semantic lens, and that we define what we describe in relation to other elements in a system—we describe what we are a part of. This barely scratches the surface of some complex (and mathematical) ideas. One might disagree with the broad application of Quine's logical theorems, but one can't deny their impact. And they make interesting thought experiments when applied to closed systems, such as digital products (https://bkaprt.com/dd46/07-06/).

Language in writing and speech

If you're interested in "what makes the Internet an interesting and unique place for language to happen," then Gretchen McCulloch's *Because Internet: Understanding the New Rules of Language* is a must-read (https://bkaprt.com/dd46/07-07/).

Peter Elbow, *Vernacular Eloquence: What Speech Can Bring to Writing*. As a content designer, it is my job to create interfaces that felt as close to speech as possible—or at least somewhere between speech and signage. An interface, unlike most other forms of writing, should feel entirely unfettered by the norms of writing conventions. Elbow's book, while not itself focused on digital interfaces, is an invaluable resource for anyone creating the words that appear in them (https://bkaprt.com/dd46/07-08/).

John Saito, "Making up Metaphors" (https://bkaprt.com/dd46/07-09/). Saito is a wonderful writer on the bridge between language and design. In this post, he offers an introduction to Lakoff and Johnson's *Metaphors We Live By*.

George Lakoff and Mark Johnson, *Metaphors We Live By* (https://bkaprt.com/dd46/07-10/). A seminal look at the prevalence of metaphor in the English language. Life-changing and incredibly obvious at the same time, this book is like turning on a microscope that shines a light on every phrase you use every day. You'll feel like a poet for days after reading it.

REFERENCES

Shortened URLs are numbered sequentially; the related long URLs are listed below for reference.

Chapter 1

01-01 https://www.bl.uk/collection-items/robert-cawdreys-a-table-alphabeticall

01-02 https://techcrunch.com/2017/01/07/on bots-language-and-making-technology-disappear

Chapter 2

02-01 https://design.google/resources/

02-02 https://m3.material.io/components/cards/specs#3f63aeba-873f-41cb-b484-020b4b131e9d

02-03 https://workspaceupdates.googleblog.com/2016/02/change-to-default-avatar-for-google.html

02-04 https://en.wikipedia.org/wiki/File:KDE-Dolphin.jpg

02-05 https://creativecommons.org/licenses/by-sa/3.0/

02-06 https://www.youtube.com/watch?v=c_KbLKm89pU&t=72s

Chapter 3

03-01 https://martinfowler.com/bliki/TwoHardThings.html

03-02 https://www.washingtonpost.com/technology/2022/04/08/algospeak-tiktok-le-dollar-bean/

03-03 https://gretchenmcculloch.com/book/

Chapter 5

05-01 https://ux.shopify.com/how-to-push-the-limits-of-a-design-system-b44fac420be

Resources

07-01 https://web.mit.edu/allanmc/www/benjamin.pdf

07-02 https://www.youtube.com/watch?v=0pDE4VX_9Kk

07-03 https://www.penguinrandomhouse.com/books/324430/ways-of-seeing-by-john-berger

07-04 https://mitpress.mit.edu/9780262539494/the-storm-of-creativity/

07-05 https://www.manss.com/en/Project/Vits%C5%93-%E2%80%93-The-Power-of-Good-Design

07-06 https://www.hup.harvard.edu/catalog.php?isbn=9780674323513

07-07 https://www.penguinrandomhouse.ca/books/540664/because-internet-by-gretchen-mcculloch/

07-08 https://global.oup.com/academic/product/vernacular-eloquence-9780199782512?cc=ca&lang=en&

07-09 https://medium.com/@jsaito/making-up-metaphors-4bcc85bc1039

07-10 https://press.uchicago.edu/ucp/books/book/chicago/M/bo3637992.html

INDEX

ABOUT A BOOK APART

We cover the emerging and essential topics in web design and development with style, clarity, and above all, brevity—because working designer-developers can't afford to waste time.

COLOPHON

The text is set in FF Yoga and its companion, FF Yoga Sans, both by Xavier Dupré. Headlines and cover are set in Titling Gothic by David Berlow.

 This book was printed in the United States using FSC certified papers.

ABOUT THE AUTHOR

 **Elizabeth McGuane** is a user experience design director and content designer who got her start in newspapers in 2003, then pivoted to UX design in 2007. Currently, she leads large, multidisciplinary design teams that include product designers, developers, researchers and content designers, solving problems in wayfinding, communication, and cross-platform design. Elizabeth divides her time between Ontario and Nova Scotia, Canada.

Printed in the USA
CPSIA information can be obtained
at www.ICGtesting.com
JSHW071949071223
53164JS00017B/79